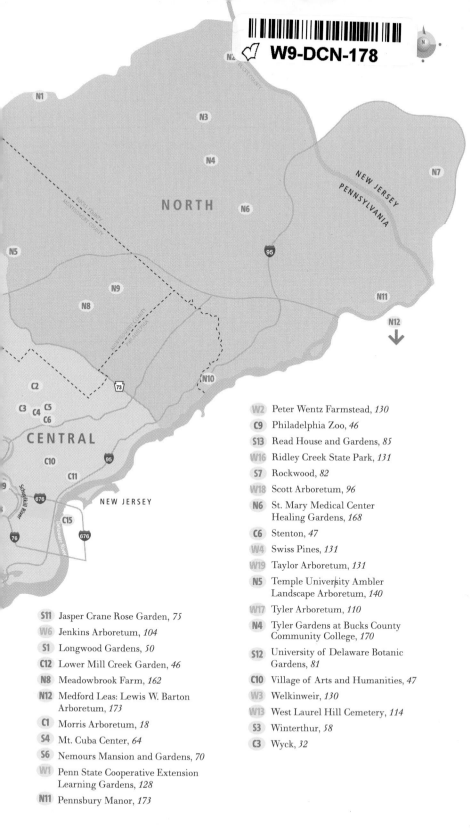

W9-DCN-178

NORTH

N1 N3 N4 N6 N7

NEW JERSEY
PENNSYLVANIA

95

N5 N9 N8 N11 N12

C2 73 N10

CENTRAL

C3 C4 C5 C6

C10 95 C11

NEW JERSEY

C15

676 676

A GUIDE TO THE
GREAT GARDENS
OF THE
PHILADELPHIA REGION

ADAM LEVINE

A Guide to the

Great
Gardens

of the Philadelphia Region

Photographs by

ROB CARDILLO

*Publication of this Guide
has been made possible
by the generous support
of the Chanticleer Foundation*

Design by
JOEL KATZ DESIGN ASSOCIATES

Temple University Press
Philadelphia

Cover: A tapestry of colors and textures at Chanticleer showcases the bold plant combinations for which this garden is world-famous.

Frontispiece: A waterlily (*Nymphaea* 'Emily Grant Hutchings') at Longwood Gardens.

Temple University Press
Philadelphia PA 19122
www.temple.edu/tempress

Copyright © 2007 by
Temple University
All rights reserved
Published 2007
Printed in Italy

This book is printed on acid-free paper for greater longevity and durability.

Library of Congress Cataloging-in-Publication Data

Levine, Adam.
  A guide to the great gardens of the Philadelphia region / Adam Levine ; photographs by Rob Cardillo ; design by Joel Katz Design Associates.
     p. cm.
  Includes bibliographical references and index.
ISBN-10 : 1-59213-510-2
ISBN-13 : 978-1-59213-510-3
(pbk. : alk. paper)
1. Gardens–Pennsylvania–Philadelphia Region–Guidebooks. 2. Philadelphia Region (Pa.)–Guidebooks. I. Cardillo, Rob. II. Title.
  SB466.U65P49 2007
  712.609748'11–dc22
          2006026042

4 6 8 9 7 5 3

CONTENTS

This book is organized geographically, with areas (Central, South, West, and North) denoted by color-coded tabs on each page. Within each geographic area, gardens are presented in order of interest to visitors (see the Introduction on pages 10–15 for a fuller explanation of the ordering). To find a specific garden, consult the table of contents, the maps on the inside front and back covers, or the index.

Fees, hours, and even features of the gardens themselves are subject to change: call ahead or check websites to avoid disappointment. A website is associated with this book: www.PhillyGardenGuide.com offers up-to-date information on garden developments and special events.

MAPS AND DIRECTIONS

The regional map (inside front cover) and the Center City Philadelphia map (inside back cover) show the approximate location of each garden in relation to the others so visitors can plan itineraries around nearby gardens. Specific driving directions can often be obtained from a garden's website or by phone. (When the directions provided by a web-based service conflict with those supplied by a garden, trust the garden.) Mass transit can be a viable and pleasant way to get to some gardens, especially for visitors willing to take a taxi or walk from the train station or transit stop. Contact the gardens for specific information.

HOURS

Some gardens have schedules that change according to the day of the week, the month, or the season. Others may be closed on certain holidays or for private events on certain days. Always call ahead to avoid the disappointment of a locked gate.

VISIT TIME

This estimate will vary depending on the visitor's pace and level of interest.

GARDEN LISTINGS

The historical background—an account of founders, explorers, designers, master gardeners, and philanthropists—precedes a description of major garden features. "Off the Beaten Path" highlights little-known or unusual aspects of the garden or nearby attractions.

ACCESSIBILITY

Touring gardens can be physically demanding. The largest gardens tend to have both paved and unpaved paths; terrain may be gently sloped or steep. Paths covered with soft materials such as gravel or woodchips may not be fully accessible for people in wheelchairs or with limited mobility, or for families with infants or toddlers in strollers.

Accessibility ratings—based on both self-reports and repeated site visits by the author—are intended to help readers decide whether wheelchair- and stroller-users and others with limited mobility will be able to cover enough of the garden to make a visit worthwhile. Call ahead for details about access to features of the garden that may be of particular interest.

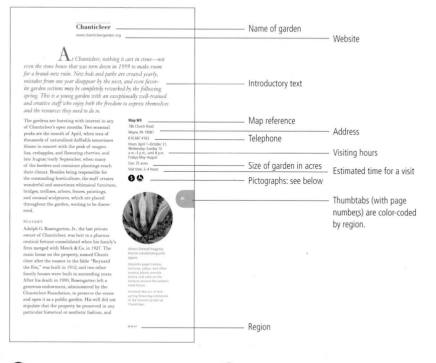

Chanticleer
www.chanticleergarden.org ———————— Name of garden
———————————————————— Website

At Chanticleer, nothing is cast in stone—not even the stone house that was torn down in 1999 to make room for a brand-new ruin. New beds and paths are created yearly, mistakes from one year disappear by the next, and even favorite garden sections may be completely reworked by the following spring. This is a young garden with an exceptionally well-trained and creative staff who enjoy both the freedom to express themselves and the resources they need to do so. ———————— Introductory text

The gardens are bursting with interest in any of Chanticleer's open months. Two seasonal peaks are the month of April, when tens of thousands of naturalized daffodils sometimes bloom in concert with the peak of magnolias, crabapples, and flowering cherries, and late August/early September, when many of the borders and container plantings reach their climax. Besides being responsible for the outstanding horticulture, the staff creates wonderful and sometimes whimsical furniture, bridges, trellises, arbors, fences, paintings, and unusual sculptures, which are placed throughout the garden, waiting to be discovered.

Map W9 ———————————— Map reference
786 Church Road
Wayne, PA 19087 ———————————— Address
610.687.4163 ———————————— Telephone
Hours: April 1–October 31,
Wednesday–Sunday 10
a.m.–5 p.m.; until 8 p.m.
Fridays May–August ———————— Visiting hours
Size: 35 acres ———————————— Size of garden in acres
Visit time: 2–4 hours ———————— Estimated time for a visit
  ———————— Pictographs: see below

99 ———————————————————— Thumbtabs (with page numbers) are color-coded by region.

HISTORY
Adolph G. Rosengarten, Jr., the last private owner of Chanticleer, was heir to a pharmaceutical fortune consolidated when his family's firm merged with Merck & Co. in 1927. The main house on the property, named Chanticleer after the rooster in the fable "Reynard the Fox," was built in 1912, and two other family houses were built in succeeding years. After his death in 1990, Rosengarten left a generous endowment, administered by the Chanticleer Foundation, to preserve the estate and open it as a public garden. His will did not stipulate that the property be preserved in any particular historical or aesthetic fashion, and

Above: Ground-hugging *festina* cohabitating with *Agave*.

Opposite page: Cannas, bananas, coleus, and other tropical plants provide drama and color on the terraces around the estate's main house.

Overleaf: Masses of late-spring-flowering *Camassia* in the Stream Garden at Chanticleer.

WEST ———————————————————— Region

 Admission free in 2007

 Regular adult admission under $8 in 2007

 Regular adult admission $8 or more in 2007

Most gardens offer discounts for children, senior citizens, and groups; some offer annual memberships or passes that include free admission. Entry fee for a garden does not always include admission to an associated house or museum or other special attractions. Consult garden websites or www.PhillyGardenGuide.com for details.

 No dedicated parking lot; street or garage parking available.

 No restrooms. In gardens associated with a historic house or museum, restrooms may not be available when the building is closed.

 Food for sale in a snack bar environment.

 Food for sale in a full service restaurant.

 Garden is associated with a historic house or a museum, which may require a separate admission fee.

 Gift shop and/or bookstore.

 Plants available for sale. In most cases this refers to special sales, held once or twice a year, at which unusual specimens can be purchased.

 Most of the garden is accessible to people using wheelchairs or with other physical limitations.

 Certain garden features are not accessible because of steep terrain, steps, soft paving, or other obstacles. Call ahead for detailed information.

 The garden is largely or completely inaccessible. Call ahead to see if special accommodations can be made.

Don't be shy. Looking at how plants grow and how they are used is a great way to learn, but a garden visit can be made far richer by engaging in a dialogue with the human creators. Most staff at public gardens enjoy talking about their work, especially if the conversation begins with a compliment.

Walk on the grass. Wander off the paths. (But stay out of the beds.) In a public garden, feel free to wander anywhere you want unless you see signs announcing that an area is off limits (such as "Staff Only"). Sometimes the most intimate and interesting garden spots are on roads and paths not usually taken. When a garden offers only guided tours, keep to the paths but let your eyes wander. Don't be afraid to direct the guide's attention to whatever you find intriguing. This will make the tour more interesting for everyone—the other visitors, the guide, and especially for you.

In every season, and *almost* all kinds of weather (see next hint), a garden has its delights and educational value. As professional garden photographers know, on gently rainy days the glistening drops of water clinging to every leaf and flower can make a garden pretty as a picture. A winter visit to one of the larger gardens, especially those with mature trees, can be enlightening and refreshing. Instead of walking at what might be called "museum pace," stopping every six feet to ogle some beautiful work of nature's art, in wintertime you can move through the garden briskly and take in the big picture—the overarching fretwork of the leafless trees, the underlying framework of shrubs, paths, and hardscape.

Both visitors and plants wilt under the noonday sun, especially in the hot, muggy summer weather of this region. On those days try to avoid being in any garden between 11 a.m. and 3 p.m. In any season of the year, early mornings and late afternoons—when the indirect, dramatic light makes colors glow—are wonderful times for garden visits.

If you want to take pictures, follow the rules of the garden. Some gardens do not allow tripods without a permit. Even where no restrictions are enforced, be respectful of the plants in search of your perfect picture. Watch where you plant your tripod, or your feet.

Leave pets at home and keep children on a leash, at least metaphorically. No matter how large the lawns are, public gardens are not playing fields. Even if an activity is not explicitly

forbidden, keep the Golden Rule in mind: Do in others' gardens as you would want them to do in yours. Plants that may have taken years to reach their peak can be destroyed in an instant by an exuberant but unthinking child; sometimes we have to do the thinking for them. Keep the kids in sight, and keep them out of the beds, trees, sculpture, and water features. Make sure they understand that flowers can be enjoyed by looking at them and smelling them and even (gently) touching them, but never picking them.

The same rules apply to adults. Do not pick, pinch, or pluck anything (even if there is an acre of it, and you have brought little envelopes or plastic bags just for this purpose, and no one is around to witness your theft). If you see a plant you covet, tell the garden staff how much you love it, and ask where they acquired it. This will be a clear hint that you'd like a piece if they can spare it. Such sharing may be forbidden in

Longwood Gardens is one of the area's most welcoming gardens for children.

some gardens, but many gardeners will gladly share a seed pod or seedling or cutting.

Watch the roads. Although the Philadelphia metropolitan region is one of the largest in the United States, it is provided with remarkably few limited access highways. As a result, those roadways tend to fill up quickly during morning and afternoon rush hours and may back up at other times if road crews are working or accidents occur. Secondary roads might actually save time and reveal far more of the character of an area than the generic superhighways.

As the horticultural epicenter of the United States, Philadelphia and the surrounding towns, suburbs, and countryside are blessed with more public gardens in a concentrated area than almost any other region in the world. Stretching from Trenton, New Jersey, through Philadelphia and down to Newark, Delaware, this area (often called the Delaware Valley) offers more horticultural riches than a visitor could possibly see even in a couple of weeks of hectic garden hopping. *A Guide to the Great Gardens of the Philadelphia Region* offers first-time horticultural visitors detailed coverage of more than 40 public gardens and information about dozens more. The book should also prove enlightening for longtime area residents, who will find new places to visit and new perspectives on old favorites.

We have arranged the book by geographic regions (see the map on the inside front cover) to help readers plan itineraries that include adjacent gardens. We provide estimated visit times

Redbud and quince frame
a view of the main house at
Winterthur.

to further aid this planning process. Within these geographic sections, we describe the gardens in order of interest to visitors, starting with those we feel have the most to offer. These decisions, made after multiple visits to each garden in 2005 and 2006 by both Adam Levine and Rob Cardillo, are based on variety, size, upkeep and design, the cost of admission, and hours of operation, as well as our intangible feelings upon visiting a place. The point of these "rankings" is to put all the gardens in their proper perspective—something previous garden guidebooks have failed to do—and thereby direct visitors to the gardens that will best satisfy their interests. By listing some of the lesser gardens we hope to bring attention to their condition and needs, and perhaps elicit support from local readers before these places disappear from the horticultural map.

All the gardens and public spaces highlighted here welcome visitors either during regular open hours or by appointment. They range in size from small city lots to estates covering hundreds of acres; in style, from formal to naturalistic; and in age, from less than 10 to more than 250 years old. We focus on ornamental landscapes and gardens because the region has such a wealth of natural areas that they could fill a guidebook on their own.

The horticultural richness of the Delaware Valley is due in part to a well-watered climate (in USDA Zones 6 and 7) that has always supported a great diversity of plants. The soil is generally fertile, and the topography of the region extends from the flat coastal plain to the varied hilly terrain of the Piedmont. Many of the region's most beautiful gardens, often associated with old estates, sit dramatically on those hillsides.

The long history of gardening in the region reaches back three centuries to the founding of Philadelphia in 1682 by Quaker leader William Penn, who dreamed of creating a "green country town" where every home would be surrounded by a garden and orchard. As the city grew and became more densely settled, property became more and more valuable and the original large lots were subdivided into tiny rectangles with little room for greenery of any kind. Residents with sufficient means escaped the crowding and unhealthiness of the city, building summer places in the surrounding countryside where ornamental gardening flourished. While a number of beautiful houses remain from this pre-Revolutionary period, only Wyck and Bartram's Garden have been able to devote significant resources to maintaining their historical landscapes.

In the 19th and 20th centuries, as Philadelphia grew into a major commercial and industrial center, wealthy merchant, banking, and manufacturing families built elaborate mansions outside Philadelphia and Wilmington, Delaware. Many of these estates rivaled English country houses in their expanse and grandeur, and they were ornamented with beautiful landscaping influenced by designs from around the world. Among the gardens from this era that are now open to the public are Andalusia, home of the Biddle family for more than 200 years; Compton, created by two Morris siblings and now called the Morris Arboretum; and Chanticleer, created by the Rosengartens, whose family chemical firm merged with Merck in the 1920s to form the largest pharmaceutical company in the world.

The gunpowder works built by E. I. du Pont in 1802 along Brandywine Creek funded the cre-

The ribbed trunk of a stately dawn redwood (*Metasequoia glyptostroboides*) at Long-wood Gardens.

ation of a horticultural empire that flourishes to this day. Du Pont family members continue to create magnificent private gardens in the Brandywine Valley, and the gardens founded by their forebears—including Longwood, Mt. Cuba, Winterthur, and Nemours—rank among the best public gardens in the country.

Though these estate gardens have many historical components and a few (such as Gibraltar) are accurate restorations of original designs, others have continued to evolve and change since they opened to the public. The horticulture at Chanticleer is particularly dynamic, and, like a number of the gardens described here, it is worth visiting again and again, even in a single season.

The Delaware Valley's tradition of botanical learning dates back at least to Benjamin Franklin's founding of the American Philosophical Society in 1743. The society promoted and published inquiries into a wide range of subjects, including horticulture and agriculture. John Bartram, an early member, was the best known of a group of colonial botanists in

Philadelphia who created extensive gardens with plants gathered from their own explorations and exchanged with other collectors in the colonies and in Europe. Horticulture and commerce came together here in the late 18th century through the efforts of the first seed merchants in America— Landreth, Buist, Dreer, and others whose names are familiar to many gardeners today.

The 1803–1806 expedition of Meriwether Lewis and William Clark to the newly purchased Louisiana Territory began in Philadelphia, and the plant specimens they collected are still housed in the city's Academy of Natural Sciences. The Pennsylvania Horticultural Society (PHS), founded in 1827, promoted discourse on horticultural topics among its members and, through annual exhibitions that began in 1829, among the general public as well. During its long history, PHS has had an incalculable and continuing impact on the horticulture of the region, most recently through its pioneering work in community gardening and greening projects and its efforts to improve many of Philadelphia's parks and public spaces.

Today, colleges, universities, and trade schools in the region offer formal programs in landscape design and ornamental horticulture, including Philadelphia's W. B. Saul High School of Agricultural Sciences. The larger public gardens and arboreta offer training and internships that attract applicants from around the world. Many national plant societies have chapters here, providing opportunities to learn about particular plants and gardening styles, including African violets, bonsai, chrysanthemums, cacti and succulents, daffodils, dahlias, daylilies, hardy plants, herbs, irises, roses, rhododendrons, rock gardening, and more. Scores of garden clubs hold regular meetings and lectures, and among their thousands of members are many who serve the public gardens as board members and volunteers. The public gardens themselves offer so many courses, conferences, lectures, tours, and other programs that it is safe to say that on almost any day of the year, especially during the peak gardening months from March through October, there is at least one educational program underway somewhere in the region. For upcoming events see www.greaterphiladelphiagardens.org and "The Wired Gardener," a monthly electronic newsletter produced by the Pennsylvania Horticultural Society and available at www.pennsylvaniahorticulturalsociety.org/garden/wired.html. The online editions of local newspapers often include gardening events in their weekly "Home" sections. In the *Philadelphia Inquirer* (www.philly.com), the "Home and Design" section, with several garden-related articles, appears on Friday.

For visitors as well as longtime residents, tapping into this "horticultural intelligentsia" will repay the effort many times over. Beyond the region's beautiful gardens, these programs provide opportunities to learn from and hobnob with some of the country's best gardeners, the folks who make this region a mecca for garden-lovers from all over the world.

Central

Morris Arboretum

www.morrisarboretum.org

Combining history and horticulture, Morris Arboretum is both a preserved estate garden and the official state arboretum, with a world-class collection of specimen plants. The peak season here is springtime, but the arboretum's many horticultural and architectural features make a visit worthwhile in any season. The trees are a special highlight, with many flowering specimens lighting up the grounds in spring, and their fall foliage providing interest in the waning months of the year.

A magnolia dominates the spring landscape on the north side of the arboretum. In the background is the restored wetland along Paper Mill Run.

Overleaf: Morris Arboretum at the height of the fall foliage season.

HISTORY

In 1881 John Morris, then in his early thirties, retired from the family business—the highly successful I. P. Morris & Co. Iron Works in Philadelphia—to pursue other activities. Like many Quakers, John and his sister, Lydia, believed in the importance of land stewardship and preservation. Both participated in many Philadelphia improvement committees, with John earning a reputation as a "champion of parks and playgrounds."

In 1887 the siblings (neither of whom ever married) purchased a tract of farmland in Philadelphia's Chestnut Hill section, over-looking Wissahickon Creek, for their summer home and gardens. From the start they saw the property, which they called Compton, as more than just a private pleasure ground and hoped it would someday become a public garden that would help people better understand the natural world. The Morrises spent more than a quarter-century and a vast amount of money developing their gardens. They corresponded with the leading horticulturists and plant explorers of the time, who eventually supplied them with over 3,500 woody plant specimens.

John died in 1915, and after Lydia's death in 1932, the Compton property (then valued at $4 million) was left to the University of Penn-sylvania. This generous donation created the Morris Arboretum, founded with the purpose of furthering scientific research, botanical education, and horticultural display.

The arboretum's plant collections grew under the leadership of various directors and cura-tors, but in the meantime the historical landscape slowly deteriorated. By 1968 the 1888 Compton mansion had to be demolished; a year later, to keep out vandals, staff boarded up the Log Cabin that John had built in 1908 as Lydia's private retreat.

In the early 1970s, board member F. Otto Haas and others involved with the institution real-ized that the arboretum had reached a turning point, and their efforts proved instrumental in bringing it back to life. William M. Klein, Jr., became director in 1977 and, with the help of curator Paul Meyer (named director in 1991), initiated a re-evaluation and total overhaul of the property that continues today.

Map C1

100 E. Northwestern Avenue
Philadelphia PA 19118

215.247.5777

Hours: Daily, 10 a.m.–4 p.m.; weekends April–October, 10 a.m.–5 p.m.; open Thursday evenings June–August

Size: 92 acres

Visit time: 2–3 hours

19

A sculpture of Lydia Morris; she and her brother, John, created the Compton estate that became the arboretum.

In the Rose Garden, some of the best rose cultivars for this region are intermingled with shrubs, perennials, annuals, and tropical plants.

Overgrown plantings were thinned; invasive shrubs and trees were removed. Vistas were selectively restored while maintaining the integrity of important specimen plants. The long list of garden structures that have been meticulously restored since the 1970s includes the Swan Pond, Log Cabin, Pump House, Mercury Loggia, Step Fountain, Rose Garden, and Fernery.

Besides this ongoing structural work, Morris Arboretum expanded its offerings of classes for adults and programs for children. Membership grew into the thousands of families, and hundreds of volunteers now do everything from manning the gift shop to weeding the beds.

An internship program attracts applicants from around the world, and arboretum staff members have participated in plant expeditions both locally and in Korea, Taiwan, and China. Arboretum publications include *The Plants of Pennsylvania*, a monumental 1,061-page illustrated manual by staff botanists Ann F. Rhoads and Timothy A. Block. In 1978 the arboretum was placed on the National Register of Historic Places, and 10 years later it was designated as the official arboretum of the Commonwealth of Pennsylvania.

THE GARDEN

Many visitors mistake the grand Victorian building that now houses the visitor center, gift shop, and education center for the original mansion. It was, in fact, the Morrises' carriage house. Until its demolition in 1968, Compton stood on the hillside where a sculpture called *Two Lines* now stands. Visitors should try to visualize this as they walk around the arboretum, since various features that seem stranded in the middle of nowhere (such as the Step Fountain) were originally placed so that they could be viewed from this now-missing building. Other features might seem oddly named, such as the Japanese Overlook, built in 1912, with an outlook point from which all views are now hidden by the beautiful trees that have matured since its creation. The arboretum's interpretive signs, many of which include old photographs, describe the original intent and focus of these features.

The color purple: *Allium* 'Purple Sensation' with the wine-colored leaves of smoke bush (*Cotinus coggygria*) in the background.

From the visitor center, where maps and other orientation materials can be obtained, a paved path encircles the arboretum and provides access for people of all abilities. Alternatively, visitors can make their own path by walking downhill from the parking lot to the Orange Balustrade, one of many eclectic landscape features influenced by the Morrises' travels in Italy, England, and Asia. This combination of formal overlook and rustic water feature is set in a grove of large trees, including several giant sequoia (*Sequoiadendron giganteum*), a beautiful paperbark maple (*Acer griseum*), and a huge Japanese raisin tree (*Hovenia dulcis*). Old and rare tree specimens such as these are found throughout the arboretum, which has more than 13,000 plants representing about 2,400 species and varieties from 27 countries. About 200 new plants are added each year.

The arboretum's most beautiful horticultural feature is the walled Rose Garden, whose four quadrants, each with a different color scheme, are planted with innovative combinations of roses, shrubs, and perennials. The

Containers featuring *Phormium* and *Petunia integrifolia* ornament a balustrade at the edge of the Rose Garden.

rose cultivars used are hardy, disease-resistant varieties, chosen after years of trials, that should do well in most gardens in the region. The Garden Railway began as a one-time display but proved so popular with children that it has become a permanent part of the garden, open from summer through early fall. The G-scale model trains run through a landscape of structures whose theme changes each year. The Mercury Loggia shelters a statue of the young winged god. John Morris built this classical structure in 1913 to celebrate his and Lydia's 25th year on the property. Walking through the grotto beneath the loggia is the most interesting way to enter the rustic Ravine Garden, a selection of mostly Asian woodland species planted along a small stream.

Above: An intense fall plant combination, with the glowing fruits of beautyberry (*Callicarpa japonica*) backed by *Amsonia hubrectii*.

Left: Old-fashioned bleeding heart (*Dicentra spectabilis*) in the Ravine Garden, with the Mercury Loggia in the background.

The Metasequoia Grove contains some of the country's oldest specimens of this beautiful tree, commonly called dawn redwood. Nearby, the Butcher Sculpture Garden offers changing exhibits of abstract and representational works. The rustic Log Cabin, once furnished with antiques and the site of Lydia Morris's tea parties, now offers visitors comfortable wooden chairs in the shade of the streamside porch. The frilly Victorian-style iron framework of the Fernery shelters a collection of ferns and related plants set amid rustic rockwork. Originally built in 1899 according to John Morris's design, the structure had deteriorated badly over the years and was restored in 1994 with the generous support of Dorrance H. Hamilton.

Swans have been a living ornament in the eponymous Swan Pond for many years.

OFF THE BEATEN PATH

A woodland path follows the banks of Wissahickon Creek to an innovative wetland-restoration project along a small tributary, Paper Mill Run.

Thursday evenings in June, July, and August are an excellent time to visit. The garden is cooler, the colors are more vibrant, and on many nights concerts are held in the Azalea Meadow.

The Chestnut Hill neighborhood, with shops and restaurants along Germantown Avenue and beautiful homes and gardens on its many side streets, is worth exploring either before or after an arboretum visit.

A leaf of *Acer pseudo-sieboldianum*, one of the arboretum's many rare tree specimens.

The Fernery is especially inviting in wintertime, when it provides a warm, green respite from the cold and monochromatic land-scape outdoors.

Bartram's Garden

www.bartramsgarden.org

From a boardwalk at the bottom of Bartram's *Garden, a visitor can look back through the trees at John Bar-*
tram's simple but exquisitely preserved stone farmhouse, a view
that has probably changed little in the past 250 years. From other
vantage points, however, evidence of the present unmistakably
intrudes: storage tanks of an oil refinery, power lines, railroad
tracks, and the tallest of Philadelphia's downtown skyscrapers.

A 200-year-old yellow-wood tree (*Cladastris lutea*) overhangs the restored seedhouse, with a garden of heirloom plants in the foreground.

Surrounded by rowhouses and industry, Bartram's Garden is the oldest surviving botanical garden in North America, as close to a horticultural shrine as exists in this country. Every visiting gardener should make a pilgrimage here to pay homage to a man whom Linnaeus himself considered "the greatest natural botanist in the world." Other than Benjamin Franklin, probably no American scientist was better known in Europe, and even today British visitors seek out the garden to honor a man who is virtually unknown in his own country.

HISTORY

"We have a botanist here, an intimate friend of mine, who knows all the plants in the Country," Benjamin Franklin wrote to his parents in 1744. That friend was John Bartram, who established one of the first botanical gardens in the United States, and certainly the most famous of its period. He purchased the land for his farm and garden in 1728 and on the property built a stone house that bears the hand-carved inscription: "It is God alone, Almty Lord, the Holy One by me ador'd."

Born in Darby, outside Philadelphia, the son of Quaker farmers, Bartram had little opportunity for formal education. He taught himself Latin and the Linnaean binomial method of botanical classification that is still used today. To expand the scope of his plant collection, Bartram corresponded with botanists and gardeners in both the colonies and Europe, exchanging seeds and plants along with information. He also sold seeds, bulbs, and plants to clients in Europe, and the money raised allowed him some freedom from farm work. Bartram's plant-collecting trips took him as far west as Lake Ontario and as far south as Florida. In 1765 he was named Royal Botanist to King George III, for which he was paid £50 a year. He often traveled with his son, William, an accomplished botanist, artist, and ornithologist. The 1791 book in which William described his travels through the American South is considered one of the finest and most readable works of its kind.

In 1812 John's granddaughter Ann and her husband, Robert Carr, established a profitable nursery on the property. In 1850 the Carrs sold the property to the wealthy industrialist

54th Street & Lindbergh Boulevard
Philadelphia, PA 19143
215.729.5281

Hours: March–mid-December, historic garden open Tuesday–Sunday 10 a.m.–5 p.m.; house open Tuesday–Sunday noon–4 p.m.

Size: 45 acres, about 8 acres of horticultural interest

Visit time: 2 hours (garden and house)

A camellia-like flower of *Franklinia alatamaha*, a late-summer-blooming tree John Bartram named after his friend Benjamin Franklin.

Andrew M. Eastwick, who built his house on adjacent land while maintaining the garden, initially with the help of a newly arrived Scottish gardener, Thomas Meehan. After Eastwick died in 1879, Meehan, by then a city councilman, got the City of Philadelphia to purchase and maintain as a park 11 acres of the Bartram property, including the core of the original garden. Although a later ordinance added 18 adjoining acres, legal complications prevented the city from taking possession of the property until 1891. By then, many of the smaller plants had been stolen; others had either died from neglect or been blown down in the "great gale" of September 1875. In 1923 the city turned the property over to the Fairmount Park Commission, which has since managed the house and garden with the assistance of the nonprofit John Bartram Association (founded in 1893).

THE GARDEN

Several ancient trees from the Bartram era (1728–1850) live on today. The most spectacular is a huge yellowwood (*Cladastris lutea*), probably planted about 1800, whose drooping white wisteria-like blossoms open around the beginning of June. Two beds close to the house feature heirloom vegetables and flowers. A native plant garden sits below the house, with a small man-made pond in the center. Several *Franklinia alatamaha* trees, named for Bartram's friend Benjamin Franklin, are planted around the property. This small tree, discovered by John and William along the Altamaha River in Georgia in 1765, is now extinct in the wild. More trees and shrubs that would have been found

In this view of the meadow (once the site of a concrete plant), a birdhouse seems to tower over the downtown Philadelphia skyline.

in Bartram's original garden will be added in the future.

John Bartram's house, built with his own hands, is an architectural landmark.

The garden contains the only piece of shoreline in the lower Schuylkill River that has never been built upon, and its only tidal wetland, created in the 1990s. A trail running along the Schuylkill River connects the wetland to the 17-acre meadow above the garden, which was planted in the 1990s on the former site of a concrete plant. At the bottom of the meadow, a boat ramp is the launching site for Schuylkill River boat tours, held occasionally during warmer weather.

OFF THE BEATEN PATH

The 1731 Bartram House has been meticulously restored and refurnished, and several 18th-century outbuildings have been creatively redesigned as offices, a gift shop, and meeting and exhibition space.

A planned recreational trail will eventually connect the garden to central Philadelphia.

Japanese House and Garden: Shofuso

www.shofuso.com

Visitors entering the house must honor Japanese custom and remove their footwear.

A jewel of the Philadelphia park system, Shofuso (Pine Breeze Villa) is one of the most beautiful recreations of a Japanese house and garden in North America, and the only house of its kind outside Japan. For flower-lovers the site is most attractive in the blush of spring bloom, but the simple elegance and meticulous authenticity of the building and landscape make it worth visiting at any time during its open season.

HISTORY

Japanese landscaping and architecture have ornamented this section of Fairmount Park since a Japanese bazaar and garden were erected for the Centennial Exhibition of 1876. Later, a 14th-century gate from a Japanese Buddhist temple stood here from 1905 until it burned in 1955.

Shofuso was a gift from the Japanese people, part of the healing process for the two countries following the horrors of World War II. A re-creation of a 17th-century upper-class residence, it was originally displayed at New York's Museum of Modern Art in 1954–1955 as an example of a traditional design with modern relevance.

In 1958 the house was given to the City of Philadelphia and reconstructed on its present site, with a garden designed by Sano Tansai. An extensive restoration of the garden was completed in 1976, and in 1982 the Friends of the Japanese House and Garden began working to manage the property. Plans call for the installation of decorative murals by Hiroshi Senju and the construction of a Japanese Cultural Center adjacent to the house.

THE GARDEN

Garden and house are inseparable here, and no visitor should miss the opportunity to tour the small *shoin-zukuri* (desk-centered) structure and take in the views of the landscape framed by its various openings. Features include a life-sized statue of Jizo, a Buddhist deity, and a stone pagoda donated by the city of Kyoto. A wooden bridge leads across a pond filled with living garden ornaments—multicolored koi that brighten the murky water. More than 200 rocks ornament the garden as well, and, along with the pond, stream, and trees, evoke the mountainous Japanese landscape in miniature.

OFF THE BEATEN PATH

Shofuso also offers tea ceremonies, gardening workshops, programs for children, and other activities. When the house and garden are closed, a beautiful view can be still obtained from the road below the pond, on North Horti-culture Drive.

A historical narrative on the Shofuso website describes the house and the reaction to its dis-play at the Museum of Modern Art.

Map C7

North Horticulture Drive, inside Fairmount Park Horti-culture Center

Mailing address: Ohio House, 4700 States Drive

Philadelphia, PA 19131

215.878.5097

Hours: May–October, Tuesday–Friday 10 a.m.–4 p.m.; Saturday–Sunday 11 a.m.–5 p.m.

Size: About 1 acre

Visit time: 1 hour (garden and house)

A meticulous re-creation, Shofuso is the latest example of Japanese archi-tecture on this Fairmount Park site; a Japanese bazaar stood here during the 1876 Centennial Exhibition.

Wyck

www.wyck.org

T*he gray gate at Wyck is one of many "portals to the past" along Germantown Avenue, where historic structures (many hidden behind modern facades) seem to be the norm rather than the exception.*

Map C3

6026 Germantown Avenue
Philadelphia, PA 19144

215.848.1690

Hours: Tuesday and Thursday noon–4 p.m.; Saturday 1–4 p.m.; also by appointment

Size: 2 acres

Visit time: 30 minutes–1 hour (garden only)

The main entrance to Wyck, one of Philadelphia's oldest and best-preserved historic houses, is adorned by the climbing rose 'Tausend-schon'.

While the staffs of nearby historic house museums have seen their gardens decline or disappear as they struggle literally to keep a roof over their heads, at Wyck both house and garden have been beautifully preserved. The garden reaches a peak in May and June, when the roses bloom, but a visit at any time will provide a momentary escape from the modern world, a reminder of a time when birdsong— not the roar of a passing city bus—was the loudest sound in this neighborhood.

History

In 1689 Hans Milan, a German Quaker, purchased the land on which Wyck now stands. In 1794 his descendant Caspar Wistar Haines moved there with his wife, Hannah, and family. Each succeeding Haines generation made changes to the house and garden. Of particular note are Jane and Reuben Haines 3rd, who created in the 1820s the formal rose garden that exists today. Their grandchildren, Jane Bowne Haines II (founder of the Pennsylvania School of Horticulture for Women, now Temple University's Ambler campus) and Caspar Wistar Haines II, maintained the gardens until 1935, but the succeeding generation of the family (the ninth) no longer lived in the house full-time, and the gardens went into a decline. In 1974, when the property was left in trust to be administered as a house museum, Ann Newlin Thompson, a horticulturist and member of the family's tenth generation, helped restore the gardens to their 19th-century appearance. Wyck was declared a National Historic Landmark in 1991.

THE GARDEN

Roses have been a feature of this simple but beautiful garden for almost 200 years. Large trees are a remnant of the property's woodlot, and smaller flowering trees and shrubs ornament various parts of the garden. Garden structures include a grape arbor added in the 1820s and a late 19th-century summerhouse. Perennial, vegetable, and herb beds contain both heirloom and modern varieties. From inside the house, redesigned in 1824 by William Strickland, dozens of windows frame beautiful views of the garden.

Roses like this hybrid perpetual, 'La Reine', have flourished at Wyck since the early 19th century.

OFF THE BEATEN PATH

The Wyck archives, open by appointment, contain thousands of objects, manuscripts, and books relating to the house, the gardens, and the Haines family. Special tours, focusing on the garden and its history, can be arranged.

Awbury Arboretum

www.awbury.org

A*wbury is a 55-acre oasis, not only for residents of the densely developed city neighborhood that surrounds it but for migratory birds and many other types of wildlife. Designed as a 19th-century pastoral landscape for the Cope family, the property features woodland, meadows, ponds, and wetlands.*

HISTORY

In 1852 Henry Cope, a wealthy Quaker merchant, purchased property in the Germantown section of Philadelphia. Originally intended as a summer retreat, the estate, which he named Awbury, eventually became the year-round residence for members of the extended Cope family. The grounds were laid out with the advice of horticulturist William Saunders, whose other projects included the National Cemetery at Gettysburg Battlefield. Concerned about development pressures, the Cope family created the arboretum in 1916 to preserve the property as open space. In 2001 the entire

Map C2

Francis Cope House

1 Awbury Road

Philadelphia, PA 19138

Entrance drive begins at
Chew Avenue north of
Haines Street

215.849.2855

Hours: Daily, dawn–dusk

Size: 55 acres

Visit time: 1–2 hours

A long driveway (opposite
page) winds through the
pastoral landscape at
Awbury, leading to the
Francis Cope House (above),
one of 33 historic structures
on the property and the
only one open to the public.

property, including 33 Victorian and Colonial
Revival structures built between 1852 and
1922, was designated the Awbury Historic
District and placed on the National Register
of Historic Places. The Francis Cope House is
open to the public; the other buildings are pri-
vately owned.

THE GARDEN

The design of the pastoral landscape can best
be appreciated on the property's main drive,
which winds uphill to the front porch of
the Francis Cope House. A four-acre "Secret
Garden" has been partially restored with support from the Garden Club of America and the
Garden Club of Philadelphia. Remote sections
of the property are set aside for a small organic
farm and a community garden.

The state champion river birch (*Betula nigra*)
grows near a spring-fed wetland that is the
only remaining above-ground section of Wingohocking Creek, the rest having been buried
in a sewer between the 1880s and 1928. This
remnant of what was once a nine-square-mile
watershed is being restored with the support
of the Philadelphia Water Department and
other government agencies. (For more on the
history of Wingohocking Creek and the city's
other underground streams, visit the Water
Department's website, www.phillyh2o.org.)

OFF THE BEATEN PATH

Awbury offers environmental education
programs for schoolchildren and teachers, a
comprehensive job-training program for young
adults, and Awbury Landscape Services, which
provides a wide range of horticultural services
and funnels profits back into the work of the
arboretum.

Camden Children's Garden

www.camdenchildrensgarden.org

O pened in 1999, the Camden Children's Garden is a horticultural playground whose mission is to provide a stimulating environment where families can experience the natural world.

Map C15

3 Riverside Drive
Camden, NJ 08103
856.365.8733
Hours: Daily, 10 a.m.–5 p.m.
Size: 4.5 acres
Visit time: 1–2 hours (for children)

Outdoor features include the Dinosaur Garden, Red Oak Run, the Storybook Garden, the Tree House, the Picnic Garden, and a Train Garden. The Philadelphia Eagles Butterfly House, the Plaza de Aibonito Tropical Exhibit, and Benjamin Franklin's Workshop are indoors. Seasonal festivals are celebrated on Saturdays, twice a month from April through November. Three amusement rides are available for a small extra charge.

The garden is operated by the Camden City Garden Club, which also sponsors educational and community greening projects and provides job training and employment for young people from the Camden area. For more on this organization, see page 182.

Kids find their own fun in this horticulturally themed playground.

Grumblethorpe

www.philalandmarks.org

Built in 1744, Grumblethorpe was home to members of the Wister family until the 1950s.

Map C4

5267 Germantown Avenue
Philadelphia, PA 19144

215.843.4820

Hours: April–December,
Tuesday, Thursday, Saturday
1–4 p.m.

Size: About 2 acres

Visit time: 30 minutes
(garden only)

An ancient *Ginkgo biloba* is
one of several majestic trees
in this small urban garden,
a remnant of a much larger
estate.

Several trees more than a hundred years old tower over the house and gardens, which include a small herb bed in back of the house and a quartet of perennial beds restored and maintained by volunteers. A successful educational program involves children from several area schools, including the John Wister Elementary School, whose asphalt playground adjoins the garden in the rear. The property is one of several administered by the Philadelphia Society for the Preservation of Landmarks.

Center City Philadelphia

(Map on inside back cover)

*S*mall gardens and landscaped parks, thousands of street trees, community gardens, and beautiful sidewalk container plantings ornament the urban hardscape and help make Center City more pleasant for visitors and residents alike. As city funds for public landscape maintenance have declined, many parks have been adopted by "Friends" organizations who volunteer time and raise money for upkeep and improvements.

Unless otherwise noted, parks and gardens in this section are free public spaces, always open, and generally flat with paved walkways. To aid those who want to take a self-guided walking tour of this area, the gardens are listed in roughly geographic order, from the banks of the Schuylkill River running southeast to the edge of the Delaware River.

Azalea Garden

Kelly Drive at Aquarium Drive, Fairmount Park

(Map C16)

The azaleas in this well-maintained and well-loved garden reach their peak of bloom in May, just in time for the many wedding parties who use the site as the backdrop for their portraits. The Pennsylvania Horticultural Society created the garden for the City of Philadelphia in the early 1950s in honor of PHS's 125th anniversary. The garden deteriorated in the 1980s, when the city cut the budget for maintenance, but in 1989 PHS joined with the Fairmount Park Commission to give the landscape a complete makeover. Spring bulbs and summer-blooming perennials and shrubs have

extended the season of interest. The Azalea Garden is adjacent to many other attractions, including Boathouse Row, the recreational trail that runs along Kelly Drive, the restored Fairmount Water Works, and the Philadelphia Museum of Art (see below).

The Friends of the Azalea Garden, a volunteer group, spend one morning a month working in the garden, and PHS holds an annual garden party here to raise money for ongoing maintenance. (For more information, contact PHS at 215.988.8800 or www. pennsylvaniahorticulturalsociety. org.) Brides and grooms should be aware that a permit from the Fairmount Park Commission (215.685.0060) is needed for photography in this garden or any other section of the park.

Philadelphia Museum of Art

2600 Benjamin Franklin Parkway (Map C17)

The 25 acres surrounding the Philadelphia Museum of Art, which is set atop a dramatic rise called Fairmount at the end of the Benjamin Franklin Parkway, had become overgrown and unkempt by the early 1990s. PHS, working with museum staff, the Fairmount Park Commission, landscape architects at Wallace Roberts Todd, the city Department of Streets, and others,

spearheaded a major renovation in the late 1990s. The grand East Courtyard and the surrounding ramparts now provide a beautiful setting worthy of this landmark building (215.763.8100; www. philamuseum.org; grounds free).

Rodin Museum

Benjamin Franklin Parkway at 22nd Street (Map C18)

Opened in 1929 to house a collection of Rodin sculptures acquired by Philadelphia movie theater magnate Jules Mastbaum, the Rodin Museum features a formal courtyard garden with a central reflecting pool, designed by landscape architect Jacques Greber.

Renovations to the garden, to be designed by the Olin Partnership, are planned (215.568.6026; www.rodinmuseum.org; open Tuesday–Sunday 10 a.m.–5 p.m.; grounds free).

Logan Square
Benjamin Franklin Parkway at 19th Street
(Map C19)

One of William Penn's original public squares, this beautiful three-acre island in the middle of a busy traffic circle was redesigned by landscape architect Jacques Greber in 1919. In 1924 Alexander Stirling Calder created the Swann Fountain, the centerpiece of the Benjamin Franklin Parkway and one of the most beautiful works of public sculpture in the United States. In 2006 PHS, in cooperation with the Fairmount Park Commission and funded by The Pew Charitable Trusts, renovated the landscape based on a plan by the Olin Partnership, replacing the beloved Empress (or *Paulownia*) trees and creating new ornamental borders featuring native plants.

Pennsylvania Horticultural Society
100 North 20th Street
(Map C20)

PHS, founded in 1827, is perhaps best known for producing the Philadelphia Flower Show. This much-anticipated extravaganza (see below) is held each March at the Pennsylvania Convention Center (215.988.8800; www.theflowershow.com). First staged in 1829, the show includes more than 50 major exhibitors, 3,000 competitive entries, and a com-

mercial sales area featuring thousands of horticultural products. The oldest and largest indoor flower show in the world, it covers 10 acres and attracts more than 250,000 visitors during its nine-day run. Thousands of flowering trees, shrubs, perennials, and annuals, forced into early bloom, create a luxuriant spectacle. Some of the best amateur horticulturists and flower arrangers in the region compete in hundreds of artistic and horticultural categories, and the quality of the entries is superlative. The show's success depends on the contributions of more than 3,000 volunteers, who do everything from long-range planning to greeting visitors on the show floor. Proceeds help fund the programs of Philadelphia Green, the community greening arm of PHS.

Less well-known is PHS's McLean Library, located on the first floor of its 20th Street headquarters. The library houses the region's most comprehensive horticultural collection, including many rare volumes and antique seed catalogues. The librarians produce "The Wired Gardener," an e-mail newsletter sent free to thousands of subscribers (viewable at www.pennsylvaniahorticulturalsociety.org/garden/wired.html). They also coordinate the volunteer experts who staff a horticultural question and answer hotline (215.988.8877; www.pennsylvaniahorticulturalsociety.org/garden/libraryhome.html; library open Monday–Friday 9 a.m.–5 p.m.).

On the sidewalk outside the library, attractive raised planters with a changing mix of shrubs, bulbs, perennials, and annuals provide color and interest year round. Across the street, at 20th & Arch Streets, the Gas Station Garden (maintained by the Logan Square Civic Association with PHS assistance) has turned an eyesore into a small but beautiful perennial garden. Up the block and around the corner, PHS worked with corporate neighbors, The Pew Charitable Trusts, SEPTA, and the Department of Streets to help transform the stretch of JFK Boulevard from 20th Street to 30th Street Station into a unified green gateway to Center City. PHS also played a crucial role in projects described elsewhere in this section; its community gardens are highlighted on pages 176–181.

College of Physicians Medicinal Herb Garden

19 South 22nd Street (Map C21)

The College of Physicians is a nonprofit educational and research institution founded in 1787 by 24 prominent Philadelphians to promote uniformity in the practice of medicine and

conduct research into diseases and their remedies. In 1911 the college created the medicinal herb garden next to its then-new building. Maintained today by the Women's Committee of the college, the garden features a variety of herbs in a four-square arrangement, with several comfortable benches for lounging and lunching. Inside the building, the Mütter Museum houses a fascinating collection of pathological and anatomical specimens and medical instruments; visitors are advised to visit the museum *before* eating lunch in the garden (215.563.3737; www.collphyphil. org; open Monday–Friday 10 a.m.–5 p.m.; garden free).

Fitler Square
Bounded by Pine, Panama, 23rd & 24th Streets (Map C22)

This attractive and shady half-acre park, created in the 1890s, features a Victorian fountain surrounded by a flower bed. Among the animal sculptures added in the 1980s are a family of turtles, a ram, and a grizzly bear. The Philadelphia Department of Recreation maintains the square with support from the Fitler Square Improvement Association (www.fitlersquare.org), founded in 1962.

Rittenhouse Square
Bounded by 18th Street, West Rittenhouse Square, Walnut & Locust Streets (Map C23)

If anything can be called a public garden in the heart of downtown Philadelphia, Rittenhouse Square is it. The six-acre square is maintained by the Fairmount Park Commission and the Friends of Rittenhouse Square (www.friends ofrittenhouse.org), a successor to the Rittenhouse Square Improve-

ment Association, which was created in 1913 to help fund a redesign by architect Paul P. Cret. The square still basically follows Cret's plan, with two main diagonal walkways, a circular outer walk, and many classical features.

The best way to enter the square is from the southwest corner, off West Rittenhouse Square, where large old trees soften the view of the skyscrapers ahead. Walking through the square on this southwest-northeast diagonal, visitors pass a semicircular bench facing a bronze goat that, like other sculptures in the park, seems to be a magnet for children. A simple bed of tough shrubs and perennials is mirrored on the far side of the walk. A rectangular plaza in the center features a pool and fountain, a Victorian guard house, and a sculpture of a lion stomping on a serpent. At the park's north-east corner, a bronze sculpture includes what is probably the only working sundial in Philadelphia. On any pleasant day the square is filled with people of all ages, sitting on the lawn and the many benches and balustrades. If the ghost of William Penn still wanders the streets of his city, he is probably sitting happily among them.

Chestnut Park

West of 17th & Chestnut Streets (Map C24)

Designed in the late 1970s by landscape architect John Collins, this small, shady, and easily overlooked park features ornamental gates, created by sculptor Christopher Ray, that are worth viewing even when the park is closed (Monday–Friday 10 a.m.– 3 p.m.).

Louis I. Kahn Memorial Park

11th & Pine Streets (Map C25)

Named for Philadelphia architect Louis I. Kahn, who lived nearby, this small corner park has been a pleasant gathering place for neighborhood residents since the 1970s. The Friends of Kahn Park (215.592.0481; http://kahnpark. tripod.com) hold events in the park, raise funds for maintenance, and have an active garden committee that cares for the shrubs, shade trees, and flower beds.

Pennsylvania Hospital Physic Garden

9th & Pine Streets (Map C26)

The Board of Managers of Pennsylvania Hospital first proposed the creation of a physic garden in 1774 to provide physicians with the raw materials for their medicines. The project was approved, but financial constraints prevented its implementation. In 1976, after a 202-year delay, local members of the Garden Club of America and the Friends of Pennsylvania Hospital planted the Physic Garden as a Bicentennial project. Designed by Martha Ludes Garra, the attractive geometric beds include more than a hundred plants used for medicines in the 18th century.

Situated in a secluded corner of the hospital grounds, the garden also provides a quiet, meditative space for hospital patients, staff, and members of the community.

The garden can be accessed directly by entering the hospital grounds from 8th Street, south of Spruce Street, and walking around the buildings to the opposite corner of the block, near 9th & Pine Streets. Visitors can also use the hospital's main entrance and follow a historical walking tour of the building that ends up in the garden. Brochures are available at the Welcome Center (215.829.6888; www.uphs.upenn.edu/paharc; open daily; call for more information).

Independence National Historical Park

The central feature of Independence National Historical Park is Independence Hall (6th & Chestnut Streets), site of the first public reading of the Declaration of Independence and, after the Revolutionary War, of the convention that drafted the U.S. Constitution. The Liberty Bell is housed nearby. The park has many open green spaces, including several of horticultural interest. **Washington Square** (bounded by Walnut Street, 6th Street, West Washington Square, & South Washington Square, Map C27), which appears on William Penn's original plan, was recently renovated with support from the Society Hill Civic Association (www.societyhillcivic. com). It contains the Tomb of the Unknown Soldier of the Revolution, a central fountain, and many grand old trees. A small recreated **18th-Century Formal Garden** (east of 339 Walnut Street, Map C28) includes an arbor and a small knot garden. **Two nearby gardens** (located on Locust Street, between 3rd & 4th Streets, Map C29) feature magnolias and roses that are especially attractive in springtime.

Philadelphia Society for the Preservation of Landmarks

This organization (www.phila landmarks.org) administers two historic houses in Society Hill, **Physick House** (321 South 4th Street; 215.925.7866; Map C30) and **Powel House** (244 South 3rd Street; 215.627.0364; Map C31). Each house has a re-creation of a 19th-century garden, and both are open for tours (Thursday–Saturday noon–5 p.m.; Sunday 1–5 p.m.; fee charged). Visitors interested mainly in horticulture can view the small gardens, featuring flowering trees and shrubs, at any time by peeking through the gates.

Irish Memorial

Front & Chestnut Streets (Map C32)

This massive sculpture by Glenna Goodacre, installed in 2003, is dedicated to the memory of more than a million Irish citizens who perished in the Great Hunger between 1845 and 1850, and to the Irish people who emigrated to the United States to better their lives. Pauline Hurley-Kurtz, a landscape architect who teaches at Temple University Ambler and is herself an Irish immigrant, created a garden setting for the sculpture with rough stone walls, hedgerow plantings, and various grasses that evoke the rugged landscape of the Emerald Isle (www.irishmemorial.org).

Also of Interest

Fairmount Park Horticulture Center and Arboretum covers 27 acres and contains a conservatory with tropical plants, a collection of specimen trees (some more than a hundred years old), and demonstration garden beds. The upkeep of the gardens varies from year to year and season to season, perhaps depending on city funding levels. Built in 1976, the center stands on the site of Horticultural Hall, the botanical display house of the 1876 Centennial Exhibition, which was damaged in a storm and demolished in 1955. (100 North Horticulture Drive, off Montgomery Drive, 19131, Map C8; 215.685.0096; www. fairmountpark.org/hortcenter. asp; grounds open daily, 9 a.m.–5 p.m. October–June; 9 a.m.–6 p.m. July–September; conservatory open daily, 9 a.m.–3 p.m.; admission free). The property also encompasses the Japanese House and Garden (see page 30), which is managed separately.

The Lower Mill Creek Garden enlivens a West Philadelphia corner with native plants in a representative meadow, wetland, and woodland setting created by landscape designer Steve McCoubrey. The University of the Sciences in Philadelphia (which owns the property), several neighborhood greening organizations, and the Philadelphia Water Department collaborated on the project, completed in 2006. This garden is one of 10 sites on the Water Department's Historic Mill Creek Trail, which traces a stream that once ran on the surface through West Philadelphia but now flows in an underground sewer. (For more information about the history of Mill Creek, see the Water Department's website, www.phillyh2o.org.) Much of the garden is visible from the sidewalk; for access call the university (43rd Street & Chester Avenue, 19104, Map C12; 215.596.8549). This garden and others have been supported by UC Green (www.ucgreen.org), which promotes greening projects throughout the University City neighborhood.

Visitors to the **Philadelphia Zoo** with an interest in horticulture will be delighted by its flowering shrubs and trees (including many large, older specimens). These are especially beautiful in springtime. Many plants are labeled, making this menagerie of plants educational as well as ornamental (34th Street & Girard Avenue, 19104, Map C9; 215.243.1100; www.philadelphiazoo.org; open daily, 10 a.m.–5 p.m.; admission fee charged).

46

Greensgrow Farms, founded in 1997 on a former industrial site in the Kensington neighborhood, is a pioneer in the urban agriculture movement. Covering an entire city block (about three-quarters of an acre), the farm uses both hydroponics and raised-bed techniques to produce a wide range of vegetables and flowering plants for area restaurants and food stores. Plants and produce are also sold to the public from early spring through Thanksgiving. Visitors are welcome during open hours, and guided tours are available by appointment (2501 E. Cumberland Street, 19125, Map C11; 215.427.2702; www.greensgrow. org; call or check website for hours).

The Village of Arts and Humanities, founded by visionary community leader Lily Yeh in 1986, transformed part of a blighted North Philadelphia neighborhood into a kind of outdoor art park. Sculpture, mosaics, and murals ornament both the streetscape and a series of garden spaces in formerly vacant lots. Visitors should call for information on guided tours (2544 Germantown Avenue, 19133, Map C10; 215.225.7830; www. villagearts.org).

The BioPond, officially known as the **James G. Kaskey Memorial Garden**, while only a remnant of the five-acre botanical garden created here in the 1890s, still provides a secluded refuge from the bustle of the Penn campus (Hamilton Walk, behind the Richards Medical Building, near 38th & Spruce Streets, 19104, Map C13; www.bio.upenn.edu/ facilities/greenhouse/biopond).

Belfield, sections of which date back to 1708, now houses the offices of the president of La Salle University. It sits amid the interesting ruins of a hillside garden created by Philadelphia artist Charles Willson Peale and subsequently modified by members of the Wister family who purchased the property from Peale in 1826 and lived there until 1984 (on 20th Street, between Belfield & Olney Avenues, 19141, Map C5; www. lasalle.edu/gen-info/farm.htm).

Stenton, in the Germantown neighborhood, was the home of James Logan, secretary to William Penn. Built in 1730, it retains a small, volunteer-tended remnant of its once grand and beautiful gardens and grounds (4601 North 18th Street, 19140, Map C6; 215.329.7312; www. stenton.org; open Tuesday– Saturday 1–4 p.m. or by appointment; grounds free).

47

South

Longwood Gardens

www.longwoodgardens.org

T*he embodiment of the dreams and fancies of one of America's wealthiest men, Longwood Gardens is one of the world's great horticultural showcases. The core of Longwood is an arboretum planted by two Quaker brothers, which industrialist Pierre Samuel du Pont saved from destruction in 1906. What du Pont, an Episcopalian, did with the rest of the property deviated greatly from the Quaker tradition of plainness and restraint, and the world's garden-lovers will be forever thankful for his extravagance.*

Overleaf: An inviting bench beneath full-blown magnolias at Winterthur.

Trained poinsettias (*Euphorbia pulcherrima*) and a spinning Christmas tree are part of Longwood's popular holiday display.

While the gardens and conservatories are of horticultural interest in every season, visitors are also attracted to Longwood's entertainments, which include fountain shows, Christmas displays, fireworks, and concerts. More than 800,000 people visit Longwood each year, so some garden or conservatory highlights may be crowded at certain times, especially on weekends and holidays. But even on the busiest days intimate, quiet spots can be found in which to sit and contemplate the beauty or listen to the birds, although the birdsong may sometimes be augmented by the chimes of the carillon, the strains of a symphony, or the brass of a Sousa march wafting over the garden.

With four acres under glass and 325 outdoor acres open to the public, Longwood has dozens of cultivated spaces, making it difficult to see everything in even a day-long visit. Visitor center staff can help plan a route around the garden and provide information on other daily activities, which can include guided tours with various themes, demonstrations, flower shows, and the above-mentioned entertainments.

HISTORY

George Peirce, an English Quaker who emigrated to Philadelphia in 1684, purchased the property on which Longwood Gardens now

Leafless bald cypress trees (*Taxodium distichum*) stand like sentries in this springtime view, with *Fritillaria* and *Narcissus* nodding over a reflecting pool.

Map S1

US 1, P.O. Box 501

Kennett Square, PA 19348

610.388.1000

Hours: Daily, November–March, 9 a.m.–5 p.m.; April–October, 9 a.m.–6 p.m.; extended evening hours in summer and at Christmastime; Monday, Wednesday, and Thursday are generally the least crowded days

Size: 1,050 acres, 325 acres open to the public

Visit time: 3–6 hours

sits. The farm eventually passed to Peirce's twin great-grandsons, Samuel and Joshua, who in 1798 began planting a garden that featured many beautiful trees. During the tenure of Joshua's son George Washington Peirce, "Peirce's Park" continued to be improved as a pleasure ground and was occasionally opened to neighbors for social events. After George's death in 1880, the family let the garden and arboretum decline and finally sold the property in 1905. It changed hands two more times before Pierre S. du Pont swooped in and bought it just as the grand old trees were about to be turned into lumber.

Having saved the trees with his timely purchase, du Pont quickly began to ornament the property around them. Many of his additions were inspired by his extensive travels in Italy and France. The great-grandson of DuPont Company founder E. I. du Pont, Pierre led the family firm in various capacities from 1902 until his death in 1954 and also served as chairman of General Motors. These two roles brought him great wealth that he both spent for his own pleasure and generously shared with others.

Between 1907 and the mid-1930s, he created numerous gardens, fountains, and the massive conservatory that is the main showplace at Longwood. Besides serving as a magnificent venue for private parties, the conservatory was also open to visitors who, then as now, were amazed by the scope of this horticultural palace.

After du Pont's death in 1954, Longwood made the transition from private estate to public garden, adding a visitor center, several garden areas (including the Palm House, which opened on Palm Sunday in 1966), and a roster of educational programs, ranging from children's classes to graduate courses, as well

Wandering off the beaten path has many rewards, including this view from behind the Italian Water Garden.

as student internships and professional gardener training. Since the late 1980s a series of renovations have been made to various garden features and sections of the conservatory.

The original 1730 Peirce farmhouse, to which Pierre added a new wing and conservatory in 1914, now houses displays highlighting the history of Longwood.

53

OUTDOOR GARDENS

The Waterlily Ponds (June–October) are one of Longwood's most unusual and spectacular displays. Specimens of the Victoria waterlily, which originated in the Amazon River basin, have platter-like floating leaves that grow to more than seven feet across and can support over a hundred pounds. This display also includes smaller waterlilies, lotuses, and other aquatic plants, and is especially beautiful at night, when the flowers are spotlit like divas onstage.

Peirce's Park is home to the 19th-century tree specimens (including several that are among the largest in the country) that prompted Pierre du Pont to buy the property. The largest of those remaining are a ginkgo and a yellow cucumber magnolia in front of the Peirce–du Pont House.

Fire and water mix in Longwood's fireworks and fountain displays, held during the warmer months. The best view is from the terrace in front of the Conservatory.

The Italian Water Garden is especially beautiful when viewed close-up from the paths below the observation deck; in late afternoon, sunlight can turn every water drop into a glistening jewel.

The Topiary Garden features shaped yews, the most popular of which represents a dog, a pig, a bear, or a bunny, depending on your point of view.

The colorful plantings along the 600-foot Flower Garden Walk (du Pont's first addition to the garden in 1907) change with the season, with bulbs in spring and bedded-out annual and tropical plants in summer.

The Main Fountain Garden, which first spouted in 1931, includes 380 water jets (the largest of which can reach 130 feet). During nighttime shows, more than 700 lighting units can tint the water any color in the rainbow. This fantastic water feature has been described as combining Italianate ornamentation, French grandeur, and World's Fair showmanship. From Memorial Day to Labor Day, evening fountain displays are choreographed to music and, several times a year, to fireworks as well. Smaller fountain shows can be seen at the Open Air Theater, also the site of theatrical and musical performances.

Displays of lilacs, wisteria, peonies, roses, and hundreds of thousands of naturalized late winter and spring bulbs are seasonal highlights in various sections of the garden.

For the outdoor Christmas Display (late November–early January), nearly half a million lights decorate the trees and shrubs in unusual patterns and designs.

Golden bleeding heart (*Dicentra spectabilis* 'Gold Heart'), a perennial. The Idea Garden also has demonstration beds of annuals, grasses, roses, vines, herbs, and other plants.

54

INDOOR GARDENS

Displays in the Conservatory change with the season. Tulips are featured in the months before spring, and thousands of specially trained chrysanthemums overflow from gigantic hanging baskets and cascade down the walls in late fall. Longwood's Christmas Tree, displayed in the Music Room, is always beautiful and always popular; expect long lines at peak times.

In the Silver Garden, designed by Isabelle Greene, silver-foliaged cacti and succulents grow amid gigantic boulders. The Cascade Garden, designed by Roberto Burle Marx and Conrad Hamerman, features 16 miniature

The yews (*Taxus sp.*) in the Topiary Garden need regular "haircuts" to maintain their neat appearance; they can be purely geometric in form or pruned into the shapes of various animals.

waterfalls cascading through a display of bromeliads and other rain forest plants. The walls of the Orchid Room are lined with plants bursting with bloom, and the long Fern Passage features a fantastic array of ferns and a small collection of carnivorous plants. Acacia, hibiscus, and roses will also be found in bloom

A gardener in hip waders removes spent blossoms from the plants in the Waterlily Garden. In the foreground are the large *Victoria* waterlilies, originally from the Amazon River basin.

in various seasons. A Children's Garden, designed by Tres Fromme, features five spaces for children to explore.

Attached to the Conservatory, the Ballroom houses the console for one of the largest organs ever built for a private residence; nearby an interesting exhibit reveals the workings of the organ, with several hands-on features and a view of some of the thousands of organ pipes.

OFF THE BEATEN PATH

Visitors staying late at Longwood for a nighttime event should take advantage of the magic light at dusk, which makes the entire garden glow. The conservatories, often open after the conclusion of these events, are worth strolling through after dark, when the plants are dramatically lit.

A collection of imposing Japanese cherry trees blooms in mid-April, on the hillside

Thousands of tulips line the Flower Garden Walk in springtime.

Bright yellow yarrow and dark blue campanula in the Hillside Garden.

beyond the Small Lake. In winter, look for the blooms of the witch hazels in the space between the Terrace Restaurant and the Peirce–du Pont House.

"Behind the Scenes" tours of areas not normally open to the public are offered a few times a year; the tour of the Main Fountain Pump House is particularly fascinating.

In dry weather electric scooters are available on a first-come, first-served basis.

Winterthur

www.winterthur.org

Winterthur is worth visiting, especially in late winter and spring, to see just one of Henry Francis du Pont's passions, its beautiful garden. But at the center of that garden looms a 175-room house harboring the other passion that makes Winterthur world-famous—du Pont's collection of antique American furniture and decorative objects. Even garden-lovers who feel claustrophobic during docent-led house tours might enjoy this one, if only for the views of the garden that this narrow structure affords from almost every room, and the insights the tour provides into the mind of the garden's creator.

Trillium grandiflorum, one of many wildflowers in the Azalea Woods.

The hilltop setting of the garden offers beautiful views in all seasons.

HISTORY

In 1816 Jacques Antoine Bidermann married Evelina Gabrielle du Pont, the daughter of his business partner, E. I. du Pont. On his retirement from the business in 1837, Bidermann and family moved from a house near the company's gunpowder works at Hagley to a 450-acre farm several miles away, which they had purchased from E. I. du Pont's estate. They called the property Winterthur (after Bidermann's ancestral home in Switzerland) and built a house on a hilltop overlooking Clenny Run, a small tributary of Brandywine

Creek. In 1867 the property was purchased and subsequently enlarged by Henry du Pont, Evelina's brother, in part to provide a future

A cherubic sculpture on the steps between the house and the Reflecting Pool, designed by Marian C. Coffin, who also planned gardens for other du Pont family members.

Map S3

Kennett Pike (DE 52)
Winterthur, DE 19735
800.448.3883

Hours: Tuesday–Sunday 10 a.m.–5 p.m.; closed Mondays except national holidays and at Christmastime

Size: 982 acres, about 60 acres of horticultural interest

Visit time: 2–3 hours (garden only)

home for his son, Henry Algernon, then serving in the army. The Colonel, as Henry A. was known, lived at Winterthur from 1875 until his death in 1926. Among a long list of business and political activities, he was a U.S. senator from 1906 to 1917.

Even before inheriting the property from the Colonel in 1926, Henry Francis du Pont made a number of significant additions to the garden: the March Bank, the initial development of Azalea Woods, and the Pinetum, inspired by similar collections of conifers he and his father had admired during a tour of England. In 1931 du Pont completed a massive nine-story addition to the house in which to display his antiques. The period rooms in the house, as well as the gardens, were opened to the public in the early 1950s. At this time du Pont and his wife moved into a smaller, 50-room residence, "The Cottage," which now houses an extensive museum shop. Du Pont continued to add to the garden and supervise its care well into his 80s, but after his death the landscape went into a slow decline. Restoration work begun in 1988 has rejuvenated the main core of the property and continues in outlying parts of the garden today.

The Garden

Set in a wooded valley surrounded by open fields, Winterthur comes to life in late winter, when early flowering bulbs and a large stand of rare *Adonis amurensis* carpet a section of woodland called the March Bank with white,

Thousands of daffodils are planted in huge drifts throughout the garden; here, a sycamore overhangs the foreground while redbud blossoms light up the background.

Scenes like this—a carpet of wildflowers beneath blooming azaleas—are commonplace throughout the garden in May.

61

yellow, and blue blossoms. In April, the Winterhazel Walk features a host of hellebores planted beneath early blooming specimens of *Corylopsis*, whose soft yellow blossoms contrast wonderfully with the bright lavender of *Rhododendron mucronulatum*. In the Azalea Woods, one of the garden's most popular features, eight acres of azaleas and rhododendrons bloom in May beneath a cathedral-like canopy of tall trees. In other sections springtime visitors will find collections of quinces, mature magnolias, peonies, crabapples, and cherries. Countless daffodils are planted in the garden and in wide sweeps in the surrounding meadows.

The woodland that looms over the center of the garden is beautiful in fall and, true to the name, even in wintertime. When viewed from the meadow above, each dormant tree appears to have been etched by a punctilious artist—a living work of art that is transformed every spring from bare twiggy grayness into a cloud of green, which, as Henry Francis du Pont said, "is one of the prettiest colors there is."

A Canada goose greets visitors to the Reflecting Pool.

Along the Winterhazel Walk, an early-spring highlight, *Corylopsis* blooms along with *Rhododendron mucronulatum*.

The Tulip Tree House in the Enchanted Woods, a favorite part of Winterthur for children and the young at heart.

Du Pont could look from his desk on the seventh floor of the house out to the elegant formal garden around the Reflecting Pool (originally a swimming pool). Designed by his lifelong friend Marian C. Coffin, this space features beautiful stonework and ironwork and a grand staircase descending several flights from the level of the house.

The newest feature at Winterthur, the Enchanted Woods, opened in 2001. Designed by Winterthur horticulturists along with landscape architect W. Gary Smith, it occupies the site of a swing set once used by du Pont's daughters. The story goes that the fairies who lived on Oak Hill missed the girls' company and created the Enchanted Woods to lure back children of all ages.

OFF THE BEATEN PATH

The Winterthur Garden Report hotline
(302.888.4856) offers recorded information,
updated frequently, on current garden highlights.

Dozens of different tours are
offered of the period rooms in
the house. Staff can help visitors choose the tour that offers
the best views of the garden.

Pronunciation hint: the "h" in
Winterthur is silent.

Looking across the Reflecting Pool at azalea time.

Mt. Cuba Center

www.mtcubacenter.org

The gardens at Mt. Cuba, created by the late Mr. and Mrs. Lammot du Pont Copeland beginning in 1935, are the region's premier showcase for the use of native plants in a woodland setting. The peak display is unarguably in spring, but the garden is beautiful all year and worth visiting at any time during its limited open seasons.

HISTORY

The 1930 wedding of Lammot du Pont Copeland and Pamela Cunningham brought together two people whose great wealth and great appreciation of the natural world seem, in retrospect, to have been destined to create a world-class garden. Lammot Copeland, a nephew of Pierre S. du Pont, creator of Longwood Gardens, was an executive of the DuPont Company and inherited his family's love of gardening as well. Pamela Copeland recalled idyllic walks with her mother in the fields and woods around her home in Litchfield, Connecticut—memories that, years later, inspired her to create her unforgettable woodland wildflower gardens.

In 1935 the Copelands purchased 155 acres of farmland on Mt. Cuba, near Greenville, Delaware, and built—on a barren hilltop—a substantial brick Colonial Revival house. To provide a sense of privacy and enclosure, they hired Thomas W. Sears, a prominent Philadelphia landscape architect, to surround the house with terraces, formal gardens, and a walled entry forecourt. At the prompting of Lammot's cousin, Henry Francis du Pont of Winterthur, they later engaged Marian C. Coffin to expand the formal gardens.

Pamela Copeland has been described as an "omnivorous" horticulturist, and her interests continued to expand throughout her long life. After the Copelands purchased 18 acres of abandoned pasture and immature woodland on a hillside adjacent to their property, she indulged a new-found passion for gardening in a woodland setting. Anticipating the eventual opening of the property to the public, in 1965 the Copelands hired landscape architect Seth Kelsey to help them develop this area into what they first envisioned as the Mt. Cuba Botanical Park, with plants from all over the world. Kelsey worked with Lammot Copeland to design the ponds that are a central feature of the garden, and he worked with Pamela Copeland to select

Map S4
P.O. Box 3570, Barley Mill Road
Greenville, DE 19807
302.239.4244
Hours: Spring and fall, tours by appointment only
Size: 630 acres, about 30 acres of horticultural interest
Visit time: About 2 hours (guided tour)

65

Opposite page: Three ponds, their banks festooned with wildflowers, reflect the passions of the garden's creators.

Below: Delphiniums and tulips in a more formal garden space designed by Marian C. Coffin.

and place plants and develop the path system that remains in use today.

After Kelsey left Mt. Cuba in 1970, the Copelands re-examined their goals. On the advice of Richard W. Lighty, professor at the University of Delaware and coordinator of the Longwood Graduate Program, they decided to focus the collection on native plants of the Piedmont region. In this densely populated stretch of rolling hills between the coastal plain and the Appalachian Mountains and running from Alabama almost to New York City, natural habitats are continually being threatened or destroyed by agricultural and commercial expansion and sprawling suburban development.

In 1983 Lighty became the first director of the Mt. Cuba Center, which works to preserve the native plants of this region and promote their use in gardens by selecting outstanding wildflower varieties to introduce into the nursery trade. By the time Lighty retired at the end of 1998, he had helped formalize thousands of records for individual plants, initiated the mapping of the collection in a computerized database, and introduced hundreds of new native plants into the garden. Lammot Copeland died in 1983. After Pamela Copeland's death in 2001, Mt. Cuba began a continuing transformation from private estate to public garden, with the gardens opened more widely to visitors and a growing number of educational programs.

Opposite page: A cascading rill leads from the lower pond, which many visitors assume is part of a natural stream system; in fact, it was created by the Copelands and landscape architect Seth Kelsey in the 1960s.

Below: Fall colors in the meadow, with a native dogwood and backlit grasses. Like all areas of the garden, the meadow needs constant maintenance.

Left: Golden club (*Orontium aquaticum*), one of a number of plants that grow on the edge of the ponds.

Right: The flowers of the spring-blooming native shrub Carolina allspice (*Calycanthus floridus*) are redolent of citrus.

THE GARDENS

Although the formal garden features designed by Thomas Sears and Marian Coffin are noteworthy, the wildflower gardens are what makes Mt. Cuba special. Visitors need to remember that just about everything here, including the trees, has been purposely planted. While many of the flowering specimens at Mt. Cuba occur naturally in this region, they would not occur in such abundance, nor would they be so perfectly groomed, without the intervention of a talented staff of gardeners. Many of the trees have had their lower limbs removed to allow more light to filter down to the shrubs and herbaceous plants of the understory. The series of four ponds, one of the garden's most beautiful features, is completely artificial. Gardeners spend about two weeks each spring mucking out the ponds, removing leaves and other debris that, in a natural setting, would eventually fill them up. The small moss garden at the base of the meadow is also intensively managed. Here a pair of tweezers is one of the gardener's tools, used to extract unwanted blades of grass from the mossy bed. In this region, with a profusion of invasive plants overrunning woodlands, meadows, and road-sides, such intensive maintenance is necessary to keep any garden from being choked with weeds.

The well-documented plant collection includes about 1,800 species and varieties of native plants of the Piedmont. The spring bloom list, densely printed in small type, ranges from *Aquilegia* to *Zephyranthes* and includes 23 species of *Trillium* and 13 species of *Rhodo-dendron*. The fall list, while shorter and not as alphabetically comprehensive, runs from *Allium* to *Vernonia* and features more than 30 varieties of asters.

OFF THE BEATEN PATH

During Mt. Cuba's annual Wildflower Celebra-tion in early May, the gardens are open free of charge for visitors to explore without a guide, at their own pace.

Above: Native dwarf lark-spur (*Delphinium tricorne*).

Bottom: A grove of white dogwood (*Cornus florida*) near the meadow.

A space used during Pamela Copeland's life-time as a cutting garden is now used for native plant varieties being tested for possible intro-duction to the nursery trade. Past introductions include *Solidago sphacelata* 'Golden Fleece', *Aster novae-angliae* 'Purple Dome', and *Aster laevis* 'Bluebird'.

Nemours Mansion and Gardens

www.nemoursmansion.org

With its magnificent 77-room mansion and astounding garden, Nemours is one of the best-kept secrets in the region. Built by Alfred Irénée du Pont between 1909 and 1932, the gardens offer one of the premier examples of the formal French style in the United States. Both house and garden are undergoing extensive renovations that will keep them closed through 2007.

The main garden axis, off the front of the house, stretches for a third of a mile. It includes a pool with 157 fountain jets, an elaborate parterre, a massive colonnade, a sunken garden, and a large lake. A Love Temple housing a life-sized Diana, one of scores of sculptures in the garden, completes this remarkable vista. Once renovations are complete,

Above: Cherubim sit atop one of the main fountains.

Opposite page: This formal garden, one of the most spectacular in the United States, includes many sculptural elements and dozens of water features.

71

this downsized homage to the gardens at Versailles will again be on a par with two other extravagant du Pont estates in the vicinity—Winterthur and Longwood Gardens, created by two of Alfred I.'s cousins.

A graceful bridge spans a stream that connects two ponds.

Delaware Center for Horticulture

www.dehort.org

The beautiful garden surrounding the head-quarters of the Delaware Center for Horticulture features exuberant plantings that continue across the street, in the parking lot, and on an adjacent railroad embankment. It represents just part of the work of DCH, which runs educational programs for children and adults, supports urban gardening and tree-planting programs, and collaborates with other agencies statewide on greening projects for parks, open spaces, and roadsides. DCH also maintains a library, runs a horticultural question-and-answer hotline, and mounts rotating art exhibits in its community gallery.

Map S10

1810 N. Dupont Street
Wilmington, DE 19806
302.658.6262

Hours: Garden open daily, dawn–dusk; center (including library) open Monday–Friday 9 a.m.–5 p.m.; Saturday 10 a.m.–2 p.m. (May–September only)

Size: About 1 acre

Visit time: 30 minutes–1 hour

A view through exuberant and varied plantings, with the woods of adjacent Brandywine Park in the background.

HISTORY

DCH was founded in 1977 by members of the Garden Club of Wilmington who wanted an organization that would offer horticultural programs in central Wilmington (see page 181). The staff and scope of the center eventually outgrew its original home in a downtown rowhouse. In 1992 DCH moved into a retrofitted 19th-century building formerly used as a residence and, later, by the Wilmington Parks and Recreation Department. The garden was created that same year. In 2002, as part of its 25th anniversary celebration, DCH dedicated a new garage, an outdoor pavilion, and a garden gate created from recycled farming and gardening equipment by sculptor Stan Smokler.

THE GARDEN

An eclectic selection of trees, shrubs, perennials, and grasses in a series of beds ornaments the original brick building and subsequent additions. Pathways and patios are paved with a variety of materials, including granite blocks that were once part of the city's streets and a mosaic of leaf-shaped terra cotta tiles created by local children. Dozens of containers showcase a wide variety of annuals, tender perennials, small trees, and other plants in

Creative reuse of recycled materials, such as the millstone, Belgian blocks, and lamppost, is a theme throughout the garden.

creative combinations. Balustrades rescued
during the reconstruction of a nearby bridge,
raised beds bordered with plastic "lumber,"
and lampposts refashioned as supports for
vines demonstrate creative ways to use recycled materials. Though it covers barely an
acre, the garden borrows a long view across
a valley into neighboring Brandywine Park,
making it seem far more expansive.

Above: Balustrades, once
part of a Wilmington
bridge, are now planted
in the garden along with
feather grass *(Stipa
tenuissima).*

Opposite page: This terrace
provides many examples of
common and exotic plants
in exciting combinations.

OFF THE BEATEN PATH

Visitors can extend a visit here by following a
path out the back of the garden and downhill
into Brandywine Park. Across Brandywine
Creek and about a half-mile downstream is
the **Jasper Crane Rose Garden** (North Park
Drive & North Van Buren Street, Map S11;
open daily, dawn–dusk; admission free). After
crossing back over Van Buren Street, the return
walk borders a picturesque mill race that once
provided water to downstream factories. This
path is part of the Northern Delaware Greenway, a recreational trail that runs for more
than 10 miles through the woods and parks of
New Castle County.

Arestored two-acre flower and vegetable garden in front of the original du Pont residence is part of a larger landscape that includes restored and ruined mill buildings in an idyllic setting along Brandywine Creek.

HISTORY

Eleutherian Mills, the original gunpowder-manufacturing works of the DuPont Company, were established here by Eleuthère Irénée du Pont de Nemours in 1802. A family residence on the hillside above the works, completed in 1803, housed several generations of the du Ponts until an explosion in the yards below drove them away in 1890. In 1921, powder manufacturing along the Brandywine ceased, and the property was sold to members of the family. In 1923 Henry Algernon du Pont purchased the ancestral home for his daughter, Louisa Evelina du Pont Crowninshield, and they restored portions of it to the property's earliest appearance. Louisa Crowninshield gave the house to the Hagley Foundation in 1952.

Archaeological excavations on the site of the garden in front of the residence provided the basis for its restoration as it may have appeared in the early 19th century. The garden that Louisa Crowninshield built below the house is now in ruins and closed to the public.

76

This formal garden reflects the French origins of the du Pont family, for whom Hagley was home for many years.

Grand trees line the mill race along Brandywine Creek, which once powered Hagley's gunpowder works.

The Garden and Landscape

The restored formal garden is composed of four quadrants featuring a juxtaposition of flowers and vegetables typical of the French style. An 1817 summerhouse rebuilt in its original location provides pleasant shelter from the summer sun. The allée of pleached (or tightly pruned) lady apple trees is not documented in garden records but is appropriate to a garden of the period.

Near the garden are several impressive trees, including a 350-year-old Osage orange (*Maclura pomifera*) with a trunk 23 feet around. "Hagley's Great Trees," a brochure available in the visitor center, enumerates 94 tree species and 18 specimens that are the largest in Delaware.

The landscape along Brandywine Creek, while not formally cultivated, is as impressive as the garden by the house. Visitors can take a self-guided half-mile tour along the creek, through restored industrial buildings, worker housing, and streamside ruins, all of which are overhung with tall trees. This scene is surprisingly peaceful and beautiful considering the deadly nature of the products once manufactured here.

Off the Beaten Path

During regular hours visitors are required to take a jitney with a guide to see the house and garden. On Wednesday evenings in July and August, from 5 to 8 p.m., this rule is relaxed and walking or biking is allowed anywhere on the property for a $1 admission fee. The house and museum buildings are closed on these evenings, but this is a perfect opportunity to see the grounds and garden.

Map S5

298 Buck Road East, P.O. Box 3630

Wilmington, DE 19807

302.658.2400

Hours: Daily, mid-March–November, 9:30 a.m.–4:30 p.m.; call for winter hours

Size: 2-acre formal garden on 235-acre property

Visit time: 1 hour (formal garden only)

SOUTH

Gibraltar

www.preservationde.org/Gibraltar

Marian C. Coffin designed Gibraltar for a wealthy Wilmington family between 1916 and 1923. The plantings look best in spring, but its formal design and many interesting sculptural features make Gibraltar one of the best small gardens in the region and worth visiting in any season.

78

Map S9
1405 Greenhill Avenue
Wilmington, DE 19806
302.651.9617 ext. 14
Hours: Daily, dawn–dusk
Size: About 2 acres (formal gardens only)
Visit time: 1 hour

HISTORY

In 1844 Wilmington businessman John Rodney Brincklé built Gibraltar, named for the rocky hilltop on which it stands. His family lived there until 1909, when Hugh Rodney Sharp and his wife, Isabella Mathieu du Pont Sharp, purchased the property and undertook extensive renovations and additions. In 1916 the Sharps hired Marian Coffin to create a formal garden. Gibraltar remained in the Sharp family until the death of H. R. Sharp, Jr., in 1990, after which it faced an uncertain future. After years of negotiation and lob-

bying, the Delaware Open Space Council
bought the property's development rights, and
the Sharp family donated Gibraltar itself to
Preservation Delaware. The garden, restored
by Rodney Robinson Landscape Architects,
opened to the public in 1999. Restoration of
the mansion is still pending.

THE GARDEN

Using gardens of the Italian Renaissance
as her model, Coffin created a symmetrical
design with a long central axis on which several dozen marble and lead sculptures serve
as ornaments and focal points. Three terrace
levels connected by a graceful marble staircase

Above: A detail of the intricate ironwork that is used
throughout the property.

Opposite page: Gibraltar
features dozens of interesting water features and
sculptures; the garden and
artwork were restored in
the 1990s.

Below: The garden's main
axis ends at this elegant,
sheltered seating area.

lead from the house down to a reflecting pool (originally a swimming pool) and into the main garden. Beyond an iron gate a less rigidly formal area features an allée of trees ending at a small temple. Here, as in many places in the garden, a comfortable garden bench invites a visitor to sit and contemplate the beautiful view.

A number of old trees remain from the original garden, but most of the plants in the garden today date to the garden restoration. Rodney Robinson and his associates carefully followed Coffin's original landscape plan (a copy of which had been preserved by the Sharp family) while renovating the pool, fountains, ironwork, walkways, and other garden features. Gibraltar is considered one of the most accurate among several re-creations of gardens by Coffin, who also designed formal gardens at Winterthur and Mt. Cuba.

A view from one of several terraces at Gibraltar. In contrast to many historic properties, here the garden was restored first; the house still awaits rehabilitation.

University of Delaware Botanic Gardens

http://ag.udel.edu/udbg

T*he University of Delaware Botanic Gardens contain a number of discrete and unusual plant collections, the oldest of which was developed in the 1950s.*

Map S12

University of Delaware
Department of Plant and
Soil Science

Newark, DE 19716

302.831.0153

Hours: Daily, 7 a.m.–dusk;
obtain permit for free
parking in Townsend Hall,
Room 113

Size: 15 acres

Visit time: About 1 hour

This teaching collection
includes many unusual
plants, including a group of
dwarf conifers.

The Emily B. Clark Garden, covering several acres in front of Townsend Hall, holds the most interest for visitors. Unusual trees and shrubs, including a dwarf conifer collection, are planted in a woodland setting. Sculptures by the university's art students are often displayed in this space as well. Besides promoting the ornamental use of plants in the landscape, the Botanic Gardens serve as a teaching aid for the College of Agricultural Sciences.

Rockwood

www.rockwood.org

A park-like setting dotted with beautiful old trees surrounds Rockwood, a mansion built between 1851 and 1854 in the Gothic Revival style by Joseph Shipley, a Quaker merchant banker. Striving to recreate the appearance of an English country estate, Shipley supplemented natural rock outcroppings with strategically situated groupings of woody plants and winding drives and walkways.

Edward Bringhurst and family, Shipley's descendants, lived at Rockwood from 1891 until 1972. The Friends of Rockwood, a volunteer group, maintained the property from the mid-1970s until 1999, when it became part of the New Castle County park system.

"Heritage Plants of Rockwood," a brochure available in the mansion, lists more than two dozen mature tree specimens, some of them state champions. Benches beneath the weeping hemlock in the walled garden and the weeping beech along the entrance driveway provide shady hideaways on hot summer days. More than 300 trees and shrubs were planted in 2002 in an effort to rejuvenate the original landscape. Climbing roses in the walled garden, blooming in May, are a seasonal highlight. The six historic acres surrounding the mansion are part of 72-acre Rockwood Park, which is itself connected to the Northern Delaware Greenway, a recreational trail that runs for more than 10 miles through New Castle County.

Map S7

Shipley Road & Washington Street Extension

Wilmington, DE 19809

302.761.4340

Hours: Daily, 6 a.m.–10 p.m.

Size: 6 acres

Visit time: 30 minutes–1 hour (garden only)

This *Ginkgo biloba* is one of the "Heritage Plants of Rockwood," some of which are more than a century old.

Goodstay Gardens

Goodstay *is most beautiful in spring, when flowering trees bloom in concert with beds of roses, peonies, and irises. The present gardens are a remnant of a much larger property that once surrounded the early 19th-century farmhouse, purchased in 1868 by Margaretta du Pont and christened Goodstay.*

In 1923 her son, T. Coleman du Pont, gave the property to his daughter, Ellen Coleman du Pont Meeds Wheelwright, as a wedding present. Ellen worked with her second husband, landscape architect Robert Wheelwright, to create the current garden configuration, with formal areas close to the house leading out to an adjacent "park" of woodland, pond, and meadow. The University of Delaware inherited Goodstay after Ellen Wheelwright's death in 1968 and now uses the house as a conference center. A magnolia walk ending in a reflecting pool, added in 1938, was renovated and replanted in 1997. The Friends of Goodstay, organized in 1993, now maintain the garden.

Map S8
Goodstay Center
University of Delaware/
Wilmington
2600 Pennsylvania
Avenue
Wilmington, DE 19806
302.573.4450
Hours: Daily, dawn–dusk
Size: About 2 acres
Visit time: 30 minutes

83

Peonies, irises, and roses (including this hybrid tea called 'Tiffany') are mainstays in this small garden.

Brandywine River Museum

www.brandywinemuseum.org

Demonstration gardens created by the Brandywine Conservancy surround the Brandywine River Museum, which features the artwork of the Wyeth family and other regional artists.

Native and naturalized flowers, trees, and shrubs of the region bloom from early spring through the first frost, though not in the masses a visitor might see in a more culti-vated garden. One of the beds in the parking lot doubles as a stormwater detention basin, an innovation when it was created in the late 1970s. This so-called pond bed provides habitat for several plant species that thrive in moist places. A bro-chure describing the plants is available at the museum reception desk, and seeds collected from the garden are for sale in the gift shop.

Above: An old millstone serves as an unusual seat near the banks of the Brandywine.

Right: *Boy with Hawk* (by sculptor Charles Park) overlooks a selection of summer-blooming plants in front of the museum.

Map S2

US 1, P.O. Box 141
Chadds Ford, PA 19317
610.388.2700
Hours: Daily, 9:30 a.m.–4:30 p.m.
Size: About 5 acres
Visit time: 30 minutes–1 hour (garden only)

Read House and Gardens

www.hsd.org/read.htm

Built in 1801 by George Read II, son of a signer of the Declaration of Independence, Read House is ornamented with a pleasant formal garden created in 1847.

Besides touring the Read House garden, visitors should stroll around adjacent historic sections of New Castle. Founded by Dutch settlers in 1651, this Delaware River town features many fine examples of 18th- and 19th-century architecture. A number of private homes have attractive gardens, some of which are open during an event held each May, "A Day in Old New Castle" (www.dayinoldnewcastle.org).

Map S13

42 The Strand
New Castle, DE 19720
302.322.8411

Hours: March–December, Tuesday, Friday, and Sunday 11 a.m.–4 p.m.; Saturday 10 a.m.–4 p.m.; weekends only in January and February

Size: About 1 acre

Visit time: 2 hours (Read House and adjacent New Castle sites)

The Read House is in the heart of historic New Castle, one of the oldest towns in the region.

West

Chanticleer

www.chanticleergarden.org

At Chanticleer, nothing is cast in stone—not even the stone house that was torn down in 1999 to make room for a brand-new ruin. New beds and paths are created yearly, mistakes from one year disappear by the next, and even favorite garden sections may be completely reworked by the following spring. This is a young garden with an exceptionally well-trained and creative staff who enjoy both the freedom to express themselves and the resources they need to do so.

The gardens are bursting with interest in any of Chanticleer's open months. Two seasonal peaks are the month of April, when tens of thousands of naturalized daffodils sometimes bloom in concert with the peak of magnolias, crabapples, and flowering cherries, and late August/early September, when many of the borders and container plantings reach their climax. Besides being responsible for the outstanding horticulture, the staff creates wonderful and sometimes whimsical furniture, bridges, trellises, arbors, fences, paintings, and unusual sculptures, which are placed throughout the garden, waiting to be discovered.

History

Adolph G. Rosengarten, Jr., the last private owner of Chanticleer, was heir to a pharmaceutical fortune consolidated when his family's firm merged with Merck & Co. in 1927. The main house on the property, named Chanticleer after the rooster in the fable "Reynard the Fox," was built in 1912, and two other family houses were built in succeeding years. After his death in 1990, Rosengarten left a generous endowment, administered by the Chanticleer Foundation, to preserve the estate and open it as a public garden. His will did not stipulate that the property be preserved in any particular historical or aesthetic fashion, and

Map W9

786 Church Road
Wayne, PA 19087
610.687.4163
Hours: April 1–October 31,
Wednesday–Sunday 10
a.m.–5 p.m.; until 8 p.m.
Fridays May–August
Size: 35 acres
Visit time: 2–4 hours

Above: Ground-hugging *Iresine* cohabitating with *Agave*.

Opposite page: Cannas, bananas, coleus, and other tropical plants provide drama and color on the terraces around the estate's main house.

Overleaf: Masses of late-spring-flowering *Camassia* in the Stream Garden at Chanticleer.

The Gravel Garden features plants that thrive in well-drained conditions, including *Agave*, columbine (*Aquilegia sp.*), thyme, and lavender.

A stone head by sculptor Marcia Donahue seems fast asleep beneath a honey-suckle vine.

this freedom has been taken to heart by the garden's staff.

Christopher Woods, Chanticleer's first director (1990–2003), transformed the commonplace estate into a series of beautiful, innovative gardens instilled with a sense of humor and drama. The gardens have continued to be refined and expanded under the current leadership of R. William Thomas.

THE GARDENS

Although Chanticleer is full of unusual plants, it is not a botanical garden or arboretum, and the dearth of plant labels and signs often surprises first-time visitors. This is mostly an aesthetic decision. As a self-proclaimed "pleasure garden," Chanticleer is a place to experience the artistry of horticulture, to wander through the wonders, to feast on the visual beauty of the colors and forms of the plants without the intrusion of words. Here the gardeners, not plant labels, are the

repository of botanical knowledge. Regular visitors soon learn that staff members are eager to share what they know, and that the information gleaned from these conversations goes far beyond what could be contained on even the largest, most conspicuous label.

The Minder Ruin is Chanticleer's version of the Sphinx, somewhat inscrutable and full of messages and meanings that are different for each visitor.

The Teacup Garden, a series of three connected courtyards behind the house at the entrance (now home to administrative offices), is a first stop for many visitors. These beds, planted with frost-sensitive tropical plants, tend to be the most variable section of the garden, changing yearly depending on the plants available and the designs of the gardener. Because of the possibility of late killing frosts in April, the Teacup (and other parts of the garden featuring tender plants) may not be fully planted until May.

The nearby Tennis Court, as its name suggests, is a former court dug up and transformed into a four-square garden in which colorful mixed plantings of shrubs, grasses, and perennial and tender herbaceous plants overflow the beds by midsummer. At the back of this garden is a pergola covered with roses and vines, beneath which a comfortable bench offers a beautiful view.

While a pond full of this lotus (*Nelumbo* 'Mrs. Perry D. Slocum') is stunning, this vigorous aquatic plant needs a drastic annual cutback to keep it under control.

91

Across an open lawn below the Tennis Court, the Cut Flower and Vegetable Garden bursts with colorful foliage, flowers, and edibles by midsummer. Toward the bottom of the property, a peaceful Stream Garden, with its wildflower beds, peaks in the spring. In other seasons it provides a cool respite from the horticultural extravagance of the other gardens.

Right: Countless thousands of daffodils are a spring highlight—in formal beds and in informal sweeps beneath a hillside of flowering trees.

Opposite page: The Chanticleer terrace, crowned with a flowering crape myrtle (*Lagerstroemia sp.*) reaches its late-summer zenith.

Below: This experimental geometric design using distinct blocks of ornamental grasses lasted only a few seasons. For now, this area has been replanted as lawn.

The Pond Garden, encompassing three ponds of increasing size and an adjacent bog garden, features colorful perennial borders and a variety of aquatic plants, including a spectacular lotus that nearly fills the largest pond

in midsummer. On a wide slope above the ponds is a large Gravel Garden, with a beautiful collection of herbs, succulents, and other plants that thrive in hot, dry conditions. Below the ponds lies the Asian Woods, a collection of mostly Asian plants beneath a very American canopy of tulip poplar, beech, and other native trees.

At the property's highest point sits the main house, Chanticleer. Around the back is a sunny terrace that is home to planted containers and beds of bulbs, perennials, and succu-

A shaft of early morning sunlight brightens the vegetable garden.

These half-submerged faces are among a number of works by Marcia Donahue in the Minder Ruin.

lents. At one end of the house is a comfortably furnished covered porch, a much appreciated shady resting spot.

Perhaps the most extravagant part of Christopher Woods's legacy is the Minder Ruin. From a design standpoint there were practical reasons to tear down Minder House, which had been the home of Adolph Rosengarten, Jr., and his wife. It stood on a prominent knoll and, being off limits to visitors, created a dead spot at the center of the evolving garden. The first idea was to "ruin" the stone house, but when that proved impractical it was torn down and a new structure and landscape were built on its footprint. Made of a gray, mica-flecked local stone called Wissahickon schist, the ruin was unveiled in 2000.

OFF THE BEATEN PATH

On the far side of Bell's Run, the stream that runs through the bottom of the property, a series of wonderful paths weave in and out

An abandoned pet head-stone finds a new home in a pathway near the Pond Garden.

The estate's former tennis court is now a colorful four-square garden. The bench beneath the pergola is one of many pieces of garden furniture built by Chanti-cleer staff.

of the edge of the woods. Other paths in the Asian Woods lead to secluded seating areas, one of them "carpeted" with terra cotta roof tiles. A more obvious attraction is an oversized sofa and armchair, complete with remote control, carved out of stone, on which any Neolithic couch potato would feel at home. Less obvious is Underwater Girl, who has been in her final resting place since 2000, unseen by most visitors. Can you find her? (Hint: she is not in the Ruin fountain; those are the Splashing Faces.)

95

Scott Arboretum

www.scottarboretum.org

Swarthmore College has never had a full-fledged department focusing on horticulture or plant science; from its inception the Scott Arboretum has been geared to the edification of the gardening public. According to a 1939 history of the arboretum, Arthur Hoyt Scott "wished to make it possible for a beginner in gardening to visit Swarthmore and see plants suitable for his own condition, rather than to see merely a beautiful picture." Beyond the plant collection, this educational goal is achieved through lectures, workshops, conferences, plant sales, garden tours, internships, garden training for volunteers, and other programs.

But in spite of Arthur Scott's utilitarian intentions, this is no staid botanical collection. The college's low stone buildings, in disparate but mostly quiet architectural styles, provide a perfect foil for luxuriant plantings in dozens of groupings and gardens. After spending hours wandering around the Scott Arboretum's horticultural wonders, any garden-loving visitors who attended colleges other than Swarthmore can be excused for considering the choice a mistake, and for wishing to go back in time and spend four years living here, on the most beautiful college campus in the United States.

History

Founded in 1869 on a tract of former farmland about 10 miles southwest of Philadelphia, Swarthmore College was close enough to the city to attract teachers but far enough away

Map W18
500 College Avenue
Swarthmore, PA 19081
610.328.8025
Hours: Daily, dawn–dusk; office and library open Monday–Friday 8:30 a.m.–noon and 1–4:30 p.m.
Size: 330 acres (entire college campus)
Visit time: 2–4 hours

97

Left: The main lawn in front of Parrish Hall offers comfortable seating and a comforting pastoral view.

Below: An extensive collection of lilacs perfumes the air in May.

to ensure that the rural setting would, in the Quaker tradition, alternately inspire, humble, and instruct the students. Few trees stood on the grounds, and planting more was an early priority. A number of those 19th-century specimens still adorn the campus today, but the college undertook no concerted efforts to

The Amphitheater (designed by Thomas Sears and John Wister), with its mature canopy of tulip poplars (*Liriodendron tulipifera*), provides a bucolic venue for graduation ceremonies and public performances.

The Terry Shane Teaching Garden incorporates innovative container plantings.

ornament the grounds until the creation of the Scott Arboretum in 1929.

Arthur Hoyt Scott (Swarthmore class of 1895), who presided over the Scott Paper Company in nearby Chester, was also a passionate amateur horticulturist who dreamed of creating a display garden where home gardeners could see a wide range of plants appropriate for this region. He initiated discussions with his alma mater in 1925 but died in 1927 before plans could be finalized. In 1929 Edith Wilder Scott, his widow, and Margaret and Owen Moon, his sister and brother-in-law, set up an endowment that created the Arthur Hoyt Scott Horticultural Foundation, dedicated to the creation of an arboretum on campus.

John Wister, considered the dean of American horticulture, served as its first director (1929–1969). In the

first 10 years, he supervised the planting of roughly 1,000 species and 4,000 varieties of trees, shrubs, and herbaceous plants, including world-class collections of magnolias, lilacs, rhododendrons, tree peonies, irises, and daffodils. Unfortunately, as the years passed, inadequate maintenance took its toll on the collections, with wind and snow storms adding to the casualties. Subsequent directors Joseph Oppe and Judith Zuk helped turn the institution around, soliciting and receiving more support from both the college administration and the community at large. Zuk launched an "arboretum assistant" program for the Scott Associates, the arboretum's dues-paying members, and these trained volunteers now devote thousands of hours each year to garden maintenance and other

The fiery autumn foliage of a Japanese maple.

tasks. The current staff, led by director Claire Sawyers, has continued to improve and expand the arboretum's plantings and educational offerings.

THE ARBORETUM

Interesting specimens, collections, and gardens are located all over the campus, which doubles as the arboretum grounds. New accessions are made yearly to a collection that now comprises more than 3,000 species and varieties of woody plants and hundreds of other perennials, annuals, and tropical plants. Almost all plants are labeled, and maps, plant lists, and other information can be found in boxes just outside the arboretum office and at various garden sites. The introductory tour brochure will lead first-time visitors to many highlights; a historic tree tour takes in several of the campus's oldest specimens. Visitors arriving at Swarthmore on SEPTA's R3 train line can enter the campus through an allée of swamp white oaks, first planted in 1879.

100

A comfortable chair over-hung with foliage and flow-ers late in the season.

In a number of areas, plants of a single genus are grouped for easy comparison. The Dean Bond Rose Garden contains more than 200 varieties that bloom from April through frost. The James R. Frorer Holly Collection, with hundreds of mature specimens donated by a college alumnus in 1973, is considered the best representation of the genus *Ilex* in the eastern United States. Other collections include lilacs, magnolias, flowering quinces, crabapples, rhododendrons, witch hazels, conifers, tree peonies, and cherries.

Many of the gardens planted since the 1990s around new or newly renovated buildings contain mixed plantings that are more typical of a home gardener's efforts. The John W. Nason Garden features plants with contrasting foliage types; this area reaches its peak in late summer and fall. The arboretum managed to preserve the Harry Wood Garden (first planted in 1959) while the Science Center was expanded around it in 2004, and added other gardens in this area as well. The Isabelle Cosby Courtyard features in-ground gardens along with containers overflowing with unusual annuals and tender perennials. More containers are located in the

With more than 200 rose varieties, the Dean Bond Rose Garden provides the flowers pinned on the college's graduating seniors.

101

garden in front of the arboretum office and in the Terry Shane Teaching Garden in back. The latter garden also features a changing annual border that can be simply beautiful or

The slopes of Wister Woods are hard to find but equally hard to forget if you visit during the height of spring.

slightly outlandish, depending on the year.

Downhill from this garden is the Biostream, where campus stormwater runoff filters through a rock-filled drainage bed surrounded by shrubs and perennials. This is one of several innovative stormwater management projects created by the college and arboretum. The largest to date collects stormwater from the Science Center and stores it in underground cisterns, where it is used for irrigation or slowly infiltrates into the ground, avoiding the type of uncontrolled discharge that, in the past, created serious erosion problems in the surrounding Crum Creek valley. A roof garden on a dormitory building is another stormwater management feature; unfortunately, this space is not open to the public.

The cathedral of towering tulip poplar trees in the Scott Outdoor Amphitheater, designed by landscape architect Thomas Sears and John Wister in 1942, provides a beautiful setting for the college's commencement exercises. Evening concerts are also held here in summertime, during which musicians onstage may find themselves competing with the roar of overhead jets, or a chorus of screaming cicadas.

OFF THE BEATEN PATH

The Wister Garden (739 Harvard Avenue, Swarthmore) was the home of director John Wister and his wife, Gertrude, from 1949 until her death in 1999. College faculty now occupy the house, but the garden the Wisters created, considered an extension of the arboretum, is open to visitors. It includes some of the largest rhododendron specimens in the entire region, a collection of tree peonies, and a hillside of wildflowers. The property can be hard to find; ask at the arboretum office for directions.

A view of the Cherry Border in mid-April.

Jenkins Arboretum

www.jenkinsarboretum.org

Created from scratch on a piece of undisturbed woodland, Jenkins Arboretum was not open to the public until 1976, and the small specimens planted back then are only now coming into maturity. Today the arboretum is the region's premier showcase for rhododendrons and azaleas, and a beautiful example of how a colorful woodland garden can be created in a naturalistic style using mostly native plants. This self-proclaimed "best kept secret on the Main Line" is at its colorful peak from April through June and holds much of interest in other seasons as well.

HISTORY

Elisabeth Phillippe Jenkins, an avid gardener and wildlife enthusiast, received a 20-acre property overlooking Valley Forge as a wedding gift from her father in 1926. After her death in 1965, her husband, H. Lawrence Jenkins, set up a foundation that would eventually begin the process of turning the property into a public arboretum. In 1971 Louisa P. Browning, a neighbor, donated her 26 adjoining acres to the arboretum (this property has yet to be opened to the public).

The Jenkinses built a house on the property, but during their tenure most of the woodland, a mixed hardwood forest with a diverse understory of native plants, remained undisturbed. The main challenge of creating a public arboretum here was installing the necessary infrastructure without destroying this fragile woodland: carefully siting a parking lot, a visitor

Two moisture-loving trees, a cottonwood and a willow, reign over the pond, which serves as both a beautiful ornament and wildlife habitat.

GREAT GARDENS

Map W6
631 Berwyn Baptist Road
Devon, PA 19333
610.647.8870
Hours: Daily, 8 a.m.–sunset
Size: 46 acres, 15 developed
Visit time: 1–2 hours

center, and a mile of paved paths, running stormwater drainage pipes, fencing the property, and digging a pond, all before any new plants could be added. After studying other public gardens and arboreta in the region, it was determined that a good horticultural niche for Jenkins would be to create an extensive collection of rhododendrons, azaleas, and other ericaceous plants, specimens of which already thrived in the property's acidic, well-drained soil. A second, broader focus is building a naturalistic landscape using North American native plants.

Top: The beauty of a pond-side *Rhododendron*—the genus that is the focus of this arboretum—is doubled in its reflection.

Bottom: A Jack-in-the-pulpit (*Arisaema sp.*) takes a seat.

The arboretum has benefited from the continuity of vision provided by its two leaders.

Leonard Sweetman served as first director until his death in 1986, after which his son, Dr. Harold Sweetman, took over the job. The father had the pleasure of implementing Lawrence Jenkins' vision of a public garden and watching it grow. The son has had perhaps the sweeter satisfaction of watching the plants, and the arboretum's reach, begin to achieve their full potential. An example of this matu-

Azalea-lovers stroll the hills in early May.

rity is one of the arboretum's hollies. When first planted, this 18-inch specimen was easy to ignore, but now it stands more than 30 feet tall.

THE ARBORETUM

Although the genus *Rhododendron* is featured here, with about 5,000 evergreen azaleas alone, the arboretum woodland is home to many

This *Hepatica* is one of many beautiful ephemeral wildflowers that line the paths in springtime.

A trail snakes through the evergreen azalea collection; the arboretum contains 5,000 specimens of this type of *Rhododendron*.

Mature trees provide shelter for a profusion of shade-loving shrubs and flowers.

other shrubs, including blueberries, spice-bush, and mountain laurel. In early spring the Woodland Walk features ephemeral wild-flowers such as trillium, trout lily, bloodroot, and other diminutive native beauties. Rho-dodendrons in this area are mostly deciduous varieties, with some early bloomers that can be surprising to see on a cold late March day, when the rest of the plants are still in their winter lockdown. Later in April and into May, Azalea Hill features a colorful collection of evergreen azaleas on the most level and acces-sible terrain in the arboretum. Elisabeth's Walk (named for Elisabeth Jenkins) features a collection of big-leaved rhododendrons that bloom from May through July.

The two-acre pond is ringed by mixed bor-ders of native shrubs, trees, and sun-loving perennials that bloom mostly in mid- to late summer; it provides habitat for a wide range of aquatic and bird life. Trout Creek begins in the arboretum, runs through the woodland at the bottom of the property, and eventually empties into the Schuylkill River.

Almost every plant has a collection label easily read from the path, and all specimens

are mapped and entered in a computerized database. The entire garden is beautifully maintained and carefully edited, as all good gardens are, but in an uncontrived, naturalistic fashion. A visitor to Jenkins might come away with a new appreciation for leaves and twigs, which are left mostly where they fall, acting as a natural weed-inhibiting mulch and, as they rot, returning their nutrients to the soil.

OFF THE BEATEN PATH

Many of the native wildflowers that edge the walkways are dormant and invisible except in the spring, so this is one place where it is especially important not to stray from the paths.

The colorful woodland canopy on a hazy autumn day.

Appointments can be made in advance for guided tours of the property around the Jenkins house and other sections of the arboretum not normally open to the public.

WEST

Tyler Arboretum

www.tylerarboretum.org

Tyler Arboretum is most beautiful in spring, when its collections of ornamental trees and shrubs burst into bloom. But the attractions here go far deeper than the surface beauty of flowers. The arboretum is a living piece of the region's horticultural history. Twenty magnificent trees more than a hundred years old, remnants of an arboretum planted by two Quaker brothers, tower over restored 18th- and 19th-century buildings. Tyler is also a place for quiet contemplation of nature, with 20 miles of woodland trails threading through its 650 acres, and its designation as an "important bird area" by the National Audubon Society.

The collection of crabapples features many cultivars, including, in the foreground, *Malus* 'Prairifire'.

HISTORY

In 1825 Minshall Painter and his brother Jacob began creating an arboretum on their family property, which dates back to a 1681 grant made by William Penn to their great-great-grandfather Thomas Minshall. In the tradition of early botanists such as John Bartram, they planted thousands of varieties of trees and shrubs, exchanged plants with other local botanists and nurserymen, and sent plants and seeds to correspondents in the United States and abroad. Neither Painter brother ever married. Well-read and learned men, they amassed a large collection of books and other items, a portion of which can still be found in the library they built on the property in 1863. Lachford Hall, occupied by Minshalls, Painters, and Tylers between 1738 and 1937, now houses a collection of the family's furniture and housewares. Both buildings are open for tours; call ahead for hours.

Laura Tyler, a member of the eighth generation, bequeathed the property to the public in 1944. John Wister, one of America's most respected plantsmen, served as the first director of the Tyler Arboretum (1946–1968) and simultaneously as director of the Scott Arboretum at Swarthmore, creating the collections of flowering trees and shrubs that remain a highlight of both institutions today.

THE ARBORETUM

About 20 of the original Painter trees, planted between 1825 and Jacob's death in 1876, survive today, forming one of the most spectacular concentrations of old trees in the region. Specimens of *Magnolia denudata*, *Ginkgo biloba*, and cedar of Lebanon (*Cedrus libani*) are among the nine state champion trees at the arboretum. Another, located on the edge of the 15-acre Pinetum, is a giant sequoia (*Sequoiadendron giganteum*) that would be even taller than its current 95 feet if sometime in the 1890s a vandal had not cut off the top to use as a Christmas tree.

Map W17

515 Painter Road
Media, PA 19063
610.566.9134

Hours: Monday–Friday, 9 a.m.–4 p.m. (winter), 9 a.m.–5 p.m. (spring to fall); extended hours on spring, summer, and fall weekends

Size: 650 acres, about 110 acres of horticultural interest

Swallowtail butterflies descend on a Joe Pye weed (*Eupatorium maculatum*) in the late-summer meadow.

111

A fall view of one of several 19th-century buildings in the arboretum. The state champion specimen of *Ginkgo biloba* looms in the rear.

The installation of fencing around Tyler's 110-acre horticultural core has enabled staff to begin rejuvenating the collections, which had been subject to repeated browsing by deer. Wister's additions here included beautiful groupings of cherries, crabapples, lilacs, magnolias, and dogwoods and 11 acres of rhododendrons, with 1,500 specimens that are just a remnant of those that Wister collected and hybridized between 1951 and 1964. In 2002 staff began an ongoing renovation of the rhododendron garden.

A small herb garden is maintained by the Philadelphia Unit of the Herb Society of America. The Stopford Family Meadow Maze appeals especially to children. Known as much for its nature-based activities as for its horticulture, the arboretum holds classes, workshops, and field trips for children and adults.

OFF THE BEATEN PATH

Across Painter Road, visitors will find Pink Hill, a serpentine barren named for the pink *Phlox subulata* that grows there in abundance. Nearby is an experimental nursery for disease-resistant varieties of the American chestnut tree. Ask at the visitor center for directions.

The herb garden.

A stone springhouse poised above Dismal Run, a Ridley Creek tributary, is one of several 19th-century structures at the arboretum.

West Laurel Hill Cemetery

www.forever-care.com

*V*isitors to West Laurel Hill Cemetery might be tempted to focus on the many celebrities among the hundred thousand people who repose here. Certainly their monuments and mausoleums add a beautiful, other-worldly (perhaps next-worldly) dimension to the landscape. But a stroll around the gravesites set among the rolling hills soon makes it apparent why this city of the dead has been a pleasant place for visits from the living for more than a century. The intricate architecture of thousands of trees provides a sheltering canopy as it carries the eye and mind skyward, softening the monumental reality of life's end and transforming a cold, inert collection of granite and marble into a beautiful garden.

Map W13

215 Belmont Avenue
Bala Cynwyd, PA 19004
610.664.1591
Hours: Monday–Saturday 7 a.m.–7 p.m. (spring–summer), 7 a.m.–5 p.m. (fall–winter); Sundays and holidays 9 a.m.–7 p.m.

Size: 187 acres

Visit time: 1–2 hours

Right top: The organic, branching framework of the trees, along with their colorful fall foliage, is heightened when viewed against the cold stonework of the mausoleum.

Right bottom: A Japanese maple seems to extend its sheltering arm over adjacent gravesites.

GREAT GARDENS

HISTORY

Laurel Hill Cemetery in Philadelphia was founded in 1836 as one of the country's first "garden cemeteries." When the creation of Philadelphia's Fairmount Park in 1867 surrounded the cemetery and prevented its further expansion, Laurel Hill managers began looking to purchase land for a new cemetery outside the city. The site of present-day West Laurel Hill was chosen for its picturesque location overlooking the Schuylkill River, hemmed in by two deep ravines that guaran-

Thousands of large and small trees ornament the cemetery's 187 acres, living tributes to the 100,000 people interred here.

teed its continued seclusion from residential development. Steamboats had carried funeral processions to the original Laurel Hill, but the managers of West Laurel Hill decided to use the railroad, which was quicker and proved popular with the public. The first burial in the cemetery occurred on May 5, 1870, and people continue to be interred here today.

THE ARBORETUM

As a certified arboretum, West Laurel Hill Cemetery has a full-time arborist among its groundskeeping staff. The cemetery grounds are especially beautiful in April and May, as the smaller ornamental trees come into bloom and the larger trees shed their winter dormancy and come back to life. In the fall, the leaves of many specimens color and drop, carpeting the graves with their ephemeral beauty. Tree specimens are remarkable for their size and number: a mature copper beech can be

awe-inspiring in any landscape; here there are more than 20 such specimens. The hilly terrain also provides vantage points from which one can see far across the landscape, taking in dozens of beautiful trees along with the architecture of the monuments. Appropriate in this land of the dead are mature specimens of so-called weeping varieties of hemlock, beech, and pine.

Maps and self-guided tour brochures focusing on architectural and horticultural features are available in the cemetery office (open Monday–Saturday 8 a.m.–4 p.m.).

OFF THE BEATEN PATH

The cemetery management welcomes purely recreational visitors, on their bikes or with their dogs, to use the 10 miles of roadways. They hold guided tours of the trees and architecture as well as other events. Call or visit the website for details.

Henry Foundation for Botanical Research

www.henrybotanicgarden.org

The Henry Foundation's wild garden is a trove of rare and unusual plants, many of them collected by Mary Gibson Henry, a self-taught botanist and horticulturist, during more than a hundred plant-collecting trips in North America. The garden reaches its peak of bloom in spring, but since Henry's goal was to have fragrant plants in flower in every month of the year, visitors will find something of interest in any season.

A sulphur butterfly feasting on an aster.

Map W10

801 Stony Lane (off Henry Lane), P.O. Box 7
Gladwyne, PA 19035
610.525.2037
Hours: Guided tours by appointment only
Size: 50 acres, about 17 acres of horticultural interest
Visit time: 1–2 hours (tour)

HISTORY

Mary Gibson Henry and her husband, Dr. John Norman Henry, bought their Gladwyne property in 1926 and moved there in 1927. Within 10 years she had amassed a collection that included more than a thousand species of woody plants. When she created the Henry Foundation in 1948, the 20-year-old garden was already world-famous for its botanical diversity.

Henry is rightly compared to John Bartram (see page 26), the 18th-century explorer whose Philadelphia garden was the most famous of his day. Like Bartram, she started her plant-collecting trips relatively late in life and with no formal training. Both filled their gardens with the rare plants they discovered and shared them with others in this country and Europe. Both constantly turned to better-known and more formally trained contemporaries for information and advice, and in the end contributed as much to horticultural knowledge as any of them.

Henry sometimes went exploring with her daughter, Josephine, an illustrator and photographer, following in the footsteps of John and William Bartram. Reading *The Travels of William Bartram*, Henry wrote, "proved to be an unending source of inspiration and, when I obtained some contemporary maps, formed the basis for planning many trips." On a 1929 quest to the southern United States, she located specimens of *Rhododendron flammeum* (then unavailable either commercially or in botanical gardens), about which the younger Bartram had written so enticingly.

A hickory tree (*Carya sp.*) nearly 100 feet tall stands by the garden entrance.

She made many subsequent trips, some with various family members, but mostly accompanied by her chauffeur and gardener, Ernest Perks, who worked for the family for more than 60 years.

119

A small woman, only an inch over five feet tall, Henry was nevertheless a dauntless explorer. On a 1931 trek to the Canadian Rockies, she was accompanied by her husband, her four children, and nine other men, with 58 horses to carry the people, tents and provisions.

The meadow surrounding this massive stone outcropping provides a hospitable environment for diverse plants.

Covering a thousand miles in 80 days, she collected numerous plants and won the largest (literally) of her many awards when the Canadian government named a peak in the region Mount Mary Henry.

Above: In concert with colorful azaleas, spring brings the blooms of blue star (*Amsonia sp.*), one of a number of genera for which the garden is known.

Below: A rare small tree, the Georgia plume (*Elliottia racemosa*).

Henry died in 1967, on her way to North Carolina in search of one more plant for the garden: *Bejaria racemosa*, commonly called tarflower. She was 83 and had already made five plant-collecting trips that year. Josephine de Nancrede Henry maintained the garden until 1996. Today, two of Mary Henry's granddaughters direct the foundation.

THE GARDEN

Instead of bedded-out annuals or fancy perennial borders, visitors here will find a naturalistic setting featuring some of the most unusual plants in the region. Some came from Mary Henry's travels across the United States and Canada; others, from the many botanists and nurserymen whom she befriended. The foundation's directors and tour guides, Susan Treadway and Betsey Davis, are her grandchildren, and their anecdotes and personal reminiscences add greatly to visitors' appreciation. As the gardens contain few paths of any sort, a visit usually involves cross-country tracks to whatever is in bloom. Depending on the season, highlights may include the many beautiful specimens of Carolina silverbell (*Halesia*), magnolias, horse-chestnuts (*Aesculus*), Stewartias, hollies, rhododendrons, and other unusual plants that have found homes in the property's many microclimates. Even in the winter, visitors may find specimens of witch hazel in bloom.

OFF THE BEATEN PATH

Artists often come here to sketch and paint the beautiful landscape, and birdwatchers do a monthly count on the property. More than 7,000 herbarium specimens from Mary Henry's travels are housed at Academy of Natural Sciences in Philadelphia (215.299.1192; www. acnatsci.org/research/biodiv/botanyvisit. html). These are part of a collection of more than 1.5 million specimens (including most of those collected during the 1803–1806 Lewis and Clark expedition), which are available to researchers by appointment.

The ivy-festooned entrance to the foundation's home is always decorated for the season.

Haverford College Arboretum

www.haverford.edu/arboretum

*T*he most impressive feature of Founders Green
on the Haverford College campus is not the staid architecture but
the monumental structure of several huge old trees. Two of them
date back to within a year of the founding of this Quaker institution and seem to embody its literal and metaphorical roots. As a
sign of their importance to the college, each has been adopted by
alumni who make monetary contributions toward its maintenance
and preservation. Unlike many other arboreta, where shrubs and
perennials are important pieces of the landscape, at the Haverford
College Arboretum the focus is truly on the trees.

122

Map W12

370 Lancaster Avenue
Haverford, PA 19041

610.896.1101

Hours: Daily, dawn–dusk

Size: 204 acres (entire college campus)

Visit time: 2 hours

HISTORY

A group of Welsh Quakers founded Haverford College in 1833, and the following year
they hired William Carvill, an English gardener, to design a landscape for the campus.
The 200-acre property consisted of the tilled
farm fields, woodlots, and pastures typical of
the rural land around Philadelphia. Carvill's
scheme, in the English pastoral tradition,
relied on new plantings of trees to both frame
and complement the open spaces, with allées
of trees to line the lanes leading up to the
college.

In 1901 Carvill's campus plan came to the attention of a group of Haverford students and alumni. They formed the volunteer Campus Club, which worked for 50 years to preserve this original landscape. That group was the progenitor of the current Campus Arboretum Association, founded in 1974, whose mission is, in part, to "maintain and build upon the diversity of the tree collection."

THE ARBORETUM

More than 1,500 trees on campus have been labeled and inventoried. Two of the oldest, located on Founders Green, are a swamp white oak (*Quercus bicolor*) and a bur oak (*Quercus macrocarpa*) that appear on Carvill's landscape plan. The campus is home to several American elms (*Ulmus americana*). New trees are regularly added to the arboretum collection, including a "class tree" planted in the autumn by each incoming freshman class.

Maps and a self-guided tree tour brochure are available at the arboretum office adjacent to the main visitors' parking lot.

OFF THE BEATEN PATH

Arboretum volunteers help maintain several garden areas, including Asian-style gardens near the dining commons and perennial beds in various places.

On the far side of the college playing fields, toward Haverford Road, an 18-acre Pinetum contains 300 specimens of conifers arranged by genus and family. The trail to the Pinetum is part of a 2.2-mile path system that encircles the campus and is popular with both walkers and their dogs.

123

Barnes Foundation Arboretum

www.barnesfoundation.org

V isitors drawn to Merion by the Barnes Foundation's world-renowned art collection are often surprised by the beauty of the surrounding arboretum. In springtime, when the panorama of flowering trees and shrubs reaches its peak, the handiwork of nature delights garden-lovers as much as the artwork inside the gallery. The main horticultural attraction at the Barnes is an outstanding collection of tree specimens, some more than a hundred years old and others rarely seen in this region.

HISTORY

Dr. Albert C. Barnes bought the 12-acre property in Merion in 1922 from Captain Joseph Lapsley Wilson, who had planted the trees that became the nucleus of the arboretum beginning in the 1880s. Besides providing an aesthetic setting for the gallery building, the

arboretum serves as a teaching collection, a mission that the doctor's wife, Laura Barnes, formalized in 1940 with the creation of the Arboretum School. To this day the school provides a comprehensive college-level horticultural education, as well as hands-on gardening opportunities, for a small group of students. The current plan is to keep the horticulture school and the arboretum at Merion, even after the artwork eventually moves to Philadelphia.

THE ARBORETUM

The arboretum's many collections include Japanese maples, magnolias, witch hazels, lilacs, Stewartias, cork trees (*Phellodendron*), and hollies (among them a cultivar named 'Laura Barnes'). Among the unusual specimens in the conifer

Map W15

300 North Latch's Lane
Merion, PA 19066

610.667.0290

Hours: 9:30 a.m.–5 p.m.;
Friday–Sunday, September–June; Wednesday–Friday, July–August. Advance reservations required; bookings up to a month ahead recommended

Size: 12 acres

Visit time: 1 hour (arboretum only)

Above: A sculptural *Stewartia*, one of several in the arboretum collection.

Opposite page: Branches etched against a blue sky: nature's artwork overhangs the main building of the Barnes Foundation.

Below: The glory of spring draws visitors out of the art gallery to view the flowering trees; the white one is *Magnolia kobus*.

125

collection are a coast redwood (*Sequoia sempervirens*), a monkey puzzle tree (*Araucaria araucana*), a China-fir (*Cunninghamia*), and an exceptionally large specimen of lacebark pine (*Pinus bungeana*). Plants of the same genus are grouped together to facilitate comparison. A wooded corner of the arboretum is underplanted with azaleas, wildflowers, and a collection of ferns, which surround a small stone teahouse overlooking a man-made pond.

The Highlands

www.highlandshistorical.org

The two-acre walled garden at The Highlands, twice nurtured and twice let go during the property's long history, is a tribute to the endurance of masonry. Each time the garden disappeared under a cloak of vines and weeds, the marvelous crenellated stone wall that surrounds the space inspired caretakers to try to recreate the beauty that once thrived there. Though simpler than it must have been in the days when a full-time gardener lived in the Gothic cottage just outside the wall, the landscape is still a pleasant ornament to the adjacent 18th-century Georgian house.

126

An herb garden (with an armillary sphere in the center) is part of the two acres enclosed by a massive crenellated wall.

Built in 1794 by Anthony Morris as a rural haven from the yellow fever epidemics that raged in Philadelphia in the late 18th century, The Highlands went through several hands before George Sheaff bought the house and adjoining farm in 1813. Sheaff, a wine merchant, added the walled garden, a grapery, and the gardener's cottage. In 1844 noted landscape architect Andrew Jackson Downing called The

Highlands "a striking example of science, skill and taste, applied to a country seat, and there are few in the Union, taken as a whole, superior to it." But by the end of the tenure of the Sheaff family in the early 20th century, the landscape had become derelict and overgrown. When Caroline Sinkler bought the property in 1917, the garden had all but disappeared.

With the help of Philadelphia architect Wilson Eyre, she restored and augmented the landscape within the walls, adding the greenhouse and numerous classical sculptures. The Pennsylvania Horticultural Society recognized Sinkler's efforts in 1933, awarding her the society's gold medal, but after her death the garden again deteriorated. In 1957 her heirs gave The Highlands to the Commonwealth of Pennsylvania, and in 1975 The Highlands Historical Society was formed to preserve, restore, and interpret it as a historic house museum. The property was placed on the National Register of Historic Places in 1976.

Restoration efforts within the walls are ongoing and have included the renovation of the greenhouse and the repair and reinstallation of sculptures from the Sinkler era. Pleasant beds of herbs and perennials have been planted close to the house, and boxwood borders have been recreated. Restoration of several outbuildings is planned.

Map W5
7001 Sheaff Lane
Fort Washington, PA 19034
215.641.2687
Hours: Daily, dawn–dusk (garden only); house tours weekdays by appointment
Size: 2 acres
Visit time: 30 minutes–1 hour

127

Above: An arched doorway leads visitors from the walled formal garden into adjacent parkland.

Below: This garden has had several incarnations. The plantings, sculpture, and structures are gradually being restored to reflect the Sinkler garden of the 1930s.

Penn State Cooperative Extension Learning Gardens

http://Montgomery.extension.psu.edu

The Learning Gardens surrounding the Montgomery County office of the Penn State Cooperative Extension Service illustrate a number of ornamental gardening styles, using perennials, herbs, grasses, annuals, bulbs, and water plants. The Universal-Accessible Garden demonstrates ways to garden with a disability and in a small space using containers, raised beds, and vertical features such as steps and trellises. As its name implies, it is completely accessible for people with physical limitations.

Map W1

1015 Bridge Road
Collegeville, PA 19426
610.489.4315

Hours: Daily, dawn–dusk;
office open Monday–Friday
8:30 a.m.–4:30 p.m.

Size: About 1 acre

Visit time: 1 hour

The Cooperative Extension Service is the outreach arm of the nation's land grant universities, of which Penn State is one. The service provides information to the general public on horticulture, agriculture, family living, financial management, nutrition, fitness, and other topics. For home gardeners, the Montgomery County office can provide a seemingly endless supply of brochures, fact sheets, and newsletters as well as answers to questions by phone or email. Through the Solution Source (1.800.617.2950 or 610.489.5158), callers can access recorded information on hundreds of subjects, many of them related to gardening.

128

Almost every county in the United States has a cooperative extension office, which can usually be found using a web search engine with the keywords "cooperative extension [county name] [state name]." Phone listings often appear under the name of the state university, such as "Penn State Cooperative Extension" or, in New Jersey, "Rutgers Cooperative Extension."

The Universal-Accessible Garden (opposite page) includes, among other features, ideas for whimsical, wheelable container plantings (above).

Also of Interest

Once the site of a large estate, the 35-acre **American College Arboretum** features large tree specimens, a pond astir with colorful koi, and Daffodil Hill, with thousands of bulbs in bloom in March and April (270 South Bryn Mawr Avenue, Bryn Mawr, PA 19010, Map W11; 610.526.1100; www.theamericancollege.edu; open daily, dawn–dusk; admission free).

At **Welkinweir**, the former estate of Everett and Grace Rodebaugh, ornamental gardens around the house give way to naturalistic areas that make up most of the 197-acre property. Now preserved by the nonprofit Green Valleys Association and listed on the National Register of Historic Places, the landscape is most beautiful in springtime, with flowering shrubs and trees in bloom. Large tree specimens and wildlife in and around a series of ponds offer interest year round. Trails from Welkinweir connect with the Horse-Shoe

Trail, with longer hikes leading to area parks, preserves, and historic sites. Guided group tours of the house and garden are available by appointment (1368 Prizer Road, Pottstown, PA 19465, Map W3; 610.469.7543; www. greenvalleys.org/welkinweir.asp; open Monday–Friday, hours vary; admission free; weekends reserved for Green Valleys Association members).

The Japanese Gardens at Pagoda 100 lie on the south side of a five-story pagoda-like office building. Conifers and cutleaf maples ornament a well-kept garden that is surprisingly serene considering its busy location. Jack Miller renovated the main garden for the current owner in 1994, and also created two smaller gardens, on the building's north side and in front of neighboring 10 Presidential Boulevard (100 Presidential Boulevard, Bala Cynwyd, PA 19004, Map W14; 610.667.1948; open daily by appointment).

Peter Wentz Farmstead, restored to reflect its appearance in the late 18th century, includes a small 19th-century-style kitchen garden (Shearer Road & PA 73, P.O. Box 240, Worcester, PA 19490, Map W2; 610.584.5104; open Tuesday–Sunday, hours vary; donation requested).

Taylor Arboretum, situated along Ridley Creek, was founded in 1931 by Joshua C. Taylor in memory of his wife, Ann. It opened to the public in 1951. Highlights include small groves of magnolias, cherries, bald cypress, and other interesting specimens (10 Ridley Drive, Wallingford, PA 19086, Map W19; 610.876.2649; open daily, 9 a.m.–4 p.m.; admission free).

Swiss Pines, a 19-acre hillside garden with Japanese elements, was created by the late Arnold Bartschi. The garden is closed on rainy days because of slippery conditions and is not accessible to people with limited mobility (20 Tree Lane, Charlestown Road, Malvern, PA 19355, Map W4; 610.935.3571 or 610.935.8795; email–swisspines@cs.com; open May–November: call for specific hours; donation requested).

The offices of **Ridley Creek State Park** are housed in the 1914 Hunting Hill Mansion, one of several park structures on the National Register of Historic Places. On a hillside above the mansion, a barely maintained formal garden with minimal plantings is still remarkable for its five terraces. Beautiful stonework, intimate walled rooms, fountains, and carved balustrades make this a diamond in the rough, begging for restoration (1023 Sycamore Mills Road, Media, PA 19063, Map W16; 610.892.3900; www.dcnr. state.pa.us/stateparks/parks/ ridleycreek.aspx; open daily, dawn–dusk; admission free).

Cabrini College sits on a 112-acre wooded campus that incorporates several structures from an early 20th-century estate, among them a mansion designed by Horace Trumbauer (610 King of Prussia Road, Radnor, PA 19087, Map W7; 610.902.8100; www. cabrini.edu).

Appleford, surrounded by a formal garden originally designed by Thomas Sears, is mainly used as a venue for weddings and other events. Garden visitors should note that a tent is permanently affixed to the front of the house between April and November (770 Mt. Moro Road, Villanova, PA 19085, Map W8; 610.527.4280; grounds open daily, dawn–dusk; admission free).

North

Grounds For Sculpture

www.groundsforsculpture.org

Surprises lurk around every bend at Grounds For Sculpture, a 35-acre sculpture garden that will delight lovers of both art and horticulture. More than 240 contemporary works of art ornament the grounds, which also feature rotating seasonal displays and two buildings for indoor exhibitions. Although the focus of the institution is clear from the name, visitors with a bias toward horticulture can easily imagine that Grounds For Sculpture is a beautiful garden in which the sculptures are just so many oversized ornaments.

GREAT GARDENS

HISTORY

In 1987 sculptor J. Seward Johnson, Jr., heir to the Johnson & Johnson company, conceived the idea of a public sculpture garden that would encourage people from all backgrounds to become more comfortable with contemporary art. The site chosen was mostly vacant land that had once been part of the New Jersey State Fairgrounds, which closed in the late 1970s.

Brian Carey of AC/BC Associates in New York City drew up the architectural and landscape plans. Three buildings that once housed fair exhibits were transformed into museum and office space and artists' studios and workshops. An oval lake, excavated from the land once occupied by the fairground's mile-long auto racetrack, also serves as a stormwater detention basin for both the sculpture park and a housing development on the opposite shore. Construction of the building and grounds began in 1989, and the inaugural exhibition was held in June 1992. The Museum Building (formerly the home of the fair's small animal exhibits) opened in May 1993.

THE GROUNDS

Visualizing this rolling, tree-filled landscape as it was in 1987, with only a few buildings and a handful of trees on ground as flat as a pancake, will help visitors appreciate the magnitude of the transformation of the site from barren former fairgrounds to a beautiful sculpture park. The ground itself could be seen as simply the largest of the many sculptures here. Before a single sculpture was placed, the flat property was contoured with small hills, valleys, and berms that create intimate settings for individual works as well as long vistas from

Above: Among the 240 sculptures on the grounds are these 1999 works by Kenneth Capps: *Equator 339°* and *Equator 183°*.

Opposite page: Modern sculpture meets horticulture throughout this wonderful garden, built on the former New Jersey State Fairgrounds.

Overleaf: Late fall in the Formal Perennial Garden at the Temple University Ambler Landscape Arboretum.

Map N7

18 Fairgrounds Road
Hamilton, NJ 08619
609.586.0616
Hours: April–October, Tuesday–Sunday 10 a.m.–8 p.m.; November–March, 10 a.m.–6 p.m.
Size: 35 acres
Visit time: 2–4 hours

135

one end of the park to the other. Ponds and artificial streams were dug, and the lake both feeds and serves as an outlet for these water features. More than two thousand trees along with thousands of shrubs and perennials are an integral part of this sculptural landscape. A number of unusual tree specimens were rescued from nearby estates or farms that were slated for development. A self-guided tree tour brochure is available at the visitor center.

The Sculpture Pad/Colonnade features a number of sculptures and two reflecting pools in several outdoor rooms separated by hedges and walls. The landscape around Rat's Restaurant includes a bridge and pond reminiscent

Above: An allée of young red maples is an evolving and growing artwork.

Right: In the foreground, *Trio* by Sarah Haviland (2001); in the background, *Tempio Bretton* by Walter Dusenbery (1981).

of Monet's garden at Giverny, with various sculptures by J. Seward Johnson that recreate famous scenes from Impressionist paintings. On one side of the Domestic Arts Building, the Courtyard provides pleasant outdoor seating, under the shade of Japanese maples, for the adjacent café. In the Water Garden on the other side of this building, a series of pools and rills flow among sculpture in a modern setting. A giant arbor festooned with wisteria originally served as a roof span for the fair's small animal building, which was shortened in its transformation into the museum.

Leucantha by Philip Grausman (1993).

Even the trees and plants are sculpted. The most interesting example is an arcing allée of closely planted red maples that form a tunnel of foliage by late spring. Some sculptures are so well hidden within densely planted groves of greenery that visitors may fail to find them on their first, or even second, visit. The appearance of the gardens and the sculpture collection changes as the backdrop of plants alters with the seasons, or even as the light shifts over the course of a day. In fall the changing leaves of the trees highlight and play off the sculpture (and vice versa). Like the best museums and the best gardens, with so much to be seen, Grounds For Sculpture is worth visiting again and again.

Off the Beaten Path

For cold-hardy visitors who want to experience a more austere landscape, perhaps on a day when the sculptures are covered by a blanket of snow, a warming hut is open in the winter months.

Signs lead the way to Grounds For Sculpture from Interstate 295, but visitors can also follow "Sculpture Along the Way," a series of monumental sculptures beginning at the highway and leading through the industrial area up to the gate of the park.

For those wishing to avoid the highway altogether, an on-site helipad is available.

138

Above: *The Couple* by John Martini (1999).

Left: *Summertime Lady* by David L. Hostetler (1999).

Temple University Ambler
Landscape Arboretum

www.ambler.temple.edu

The gardens of the Landscape Arboretum at Temple University Ambler add a rural feel to this suburban campus, reflecting the institution's origins as a working farm that was transformed into the Pennsylvania School of Horticulture for Women. Old and new gardens provide students (now men along with women) with examples of both classic landscape architecture and designs based on modern ecological principles. Visitors will find areas of interest from spring through fall, with beautiful formal perennial borders reaching their peak in late August and September.

Map N5

580 Meetinghouse Road
Ambler, PA 19002
267.468.8400
Hours: Daily, dawn–dusk
Size: 187 acres, about 10 acres of horticultural interest
Visit time: 1–2 hours

Grasses go tan, and blue star (*Amsonia sp.*) turns yellow in this fall border.

HISTORY

In 1910 Jane Bowne Haines II, along with colleagues and former classmates from Bryn Mawr College, founded the Pennsylvania School of Horticulture for Women on a 71-acre farm in Ambler, north of Philadelphia. One of their goals was to broaden career opportunities for women.

For each hour spent in the lecture halls, students received two hours of hands-on training in the gardens and fields. As proper gentlewoman "farmerettes," they wore dark tunics, skirts, white shirts, and high-top boots. Perhaps the propriety of this uniform convinced the Philadelphia elite that the school might be appropriate for their debutante daughters. Louise Carter Bush-Brown, a 1916 graduate, led the school during its most successful years (1924–1952) as new classrooms and dormito-

Ferns, wild columbine (*Aquilegia canadensis*), and coral bells (*Heuchera sp.*) catch the late afternoon light in this spring view of the Native Plant Garden.

Below: Fall color on a leaf of the fullmoon maple (*Acer japonicum*); new growth in the spring is a luscious, luminous green.

141

ries were built, 116 acres were added to the campus, and the school attracted applicants even from overseas.

In 1958 the school became part of Temple University, and it now offers undergraduate degree programs in several areas. A Department of Landscape Architecture and Horticulture was established in 1988, and in 2000 the university officially designated the campus as an arboretum.

THE ARBORETUM

The gardens cover a range of styles, with both formal and naturalistic areas. Ecologically sensitive landscape design is a growing area of interest, spurred by the University's Center for Sustainable Communities (www.temple.edu/ambler/csc), which is based on the Ambler campus. The arboretum serves as an outdoor classroom and teaching aid as well as a place where horticulture and landscape design students can get hands-on experience.

A series of gardens around Dixon Hall form the core of the arboretum. In a Woodland Garden, planted in the 1920s, visitors will find flowering trees and bulbs in springtime and a shady retreat in the summer and fall. A Native Plant Garden demonstrates that these subtle beauties can be effectively used in a formal design. The area also includes an Herb Garden and a Groundcover Garden, designed and built by students in the 1990s, and the Louise Stine Fisher Garden, featuring a collection of dwarf evergreens and Japanese maples in an intimate setting.

The pink form of the native dogwood (*Cornus florida*).

142

The centerpiece is the Formal Perennial Garden, designed in 1931 by landscape architect Beatrix Farrand and James Bush-Brown, a design instructor and husband of the school's director. From the back of Dixon Hall steps lead down to a grass path between two overflowing English-style borders, with an arborvitae hedge providing a dark backdrop for the colorful palette of perennials. Two garden houses opposite the steps provide a focal point and a shady seating area that overlooks both the perennial borders and the woodland behind it. The borders were renovated in 1998 by Stephanie Cohen and Rudolph Keller, who retained the formal outline of the beds but replanted them with modern varieties.

143

Daylilies (*Hemerocallis sp.*), lamb's ear (*Stachys sp.*), hostas, and other low-growing plants in the Groundcover Garden.

In the Sustainable Wetland Garden, stormwater runoff from various sources pools up before filtering back into the ground. A lush selection of moisture-loving plants gives this area a jungle-like atmosphere by midsummer. Students originally created this garden's pergola and crushed-glass paving stones for the school's exhibit at the 1997 Philadelphia Flower Show.

A garden with plants of winter interest, a conifer garden, and a student-designed labyrinth (first exhibited at the 2006 Philadelphia Flower Show) are now in the planning stages.

Above: The seeds of butter-fly weed (*Asclepias tuberosa*), with their downy attachments, can be carried away by the slightest breeze.

Right: The fully developed flower of *Clematis integrifolia* seems to shelter an unopened bud.

OFF THE BEATEN PATH

In 2005 a demonstration "green roof," meant to decrease both stormwater runoff and cooling costs, was installed on the Intercollegiate Athletic Building. The roof is partially visible from ground level, and rooftop tours can be arranged.

Informative display panels in the lobby of Dixon Hall cover the history of the campus, area garden clubs, and local women in horticulture.

Hortulus Farm Gardens

www.hortulusfarm.com

*A*t *Hortulus Farm Gardens, simple 18th- and 19th-century buildings are surrounded by such horticultural opulence that the scene registers as both sublimely serene and surreal. This is horticulture on hyperdrive. Huge clumps of hostas line a grassy walk down into the garden. An oversized planted urn looms at the end of a long allée. Not just one or three but a regiment of fat and happy dwarf Alberta spruces ornament steps leading into one of the gardens. Fowl wander freely, their clucks, quacks, and honks adding to the exuberance of the scene. Hortulus Farm is a horticultural showcase worth visiting anytime during its open months.*

An early-spring view, showing bare vines that will soon envelop this pergola with a canopy of foliage.

HISTORY

Descendants of the Thompson and Warner families ran a large dairy operation on the property from the 18th century into the 20th. The old stone farmhouse dates from 1723, with additions made into the 1790s; it was added

A detail of the lush Perennial Borders.

to the National Register of Historic Places in 2004. Several farm buildings date from the 1820s. Sold during the Depression at a sheriff's sale, the farm went through many hands before Renny Reynolds, the garden and event designer, and Jack Staub, radio personality and garden author, purchased the property in 1980. They immediately began renovating the buildings and carving gardens from the overgrown pastures and woodland, a process that is still underway. In 2000 they created the Hortulus Farm Foundation to ensure the preservation of the property and open it more widely to the public.

THE GARDENS

Wherever a visitor looks on this wonderful and whimsical gentlemen's farm, diverse plants are consorting in more than 20 discrete gardens, making the property seem like a horticultural version of a 1960s love-in. Dramatic vistas abound. The most exciting ends at the garden's central feature, the circular Pool Garden, which is surrounded by striking beds overflowing with purple and yellow foliage and flowers. Several small streams run through the property, on opposite sides of a pond on which paddling waterfowl add a picturesque touch. The farm includes a French Garden with

Map N3

60 Thompson Mill Road

Wrightstown, PA 18940

215.598.0550

Hours: May–October, guided tours by appointment only; several open days scheduled through The Garden Conservancy (see page 182)

Size: 30 acres

Visit time: 2 hours (guided tour)

147

These black swans are among dozens of exotic and domesticated fowl that reside on the farm.

clipped hedges; an Italian Fountain garden; a circular White Garden; richly planted Perennial Borders; a woodland with 200,000 spring-blooming bulbs; and immaculately maintained raised beds in the Kitchen Garden. Even with this abundance, Reynolds and Staub are far from finished, planning more new spaces and refinements to existing plantings. A friend recently purchased the adjoining 30-acre property, which, like Hortulus Farm, has been preserved in perpetuity; gardens may eventually spill over into that property as well.

OFF THE BEATEN PATH

In 2006 Reynolds and Staub gave Hortulus Farm Nursery, adjacent to the gardens, to the Heritage Conservancy (www.heritageconservancy.org), a Bucks County land preservation organization. Profits from nursery sales will help fund the gardens and the Conservancy's wide-ranging conservation efforts.

The entrance to an herb and vegetable garden is punctuated with topiary dwarf spruces and bordered by boxwood and hostas.

149

Andalusia

S et on the Delaware River about 13 miles upstream from central Philadelphia, Andalusia is best known for its historic buildings and the collection of art and antiques amassed during the tenure of the Craig and Biddle families, who have occupied the estate since 1795.

Map N10

1237 State Road,
P.O. Box 158

Andalusia, PA 19020

215.245.5479

Hours: Group tours by appointment only

Size: About 90 acres

Visit time: 2 hours (garden and house tour)

Wisteria on one of the Grapery walls. This massive structure is a remnant of Nicholas Biddle's hothouse viticulture venture, begun in the 1830s.

The estate is also an intact historical landscape, rare for this region, with buildings, gardens, and even views that look much as they did in the 19th century. The gardens are especially beautiful in spring, but a walk through the grounds at any time of year is worthwhile. Accompanied by the crunch of gravel underfoot and birdsong overhead, the peacefulness can be trance-inducing. As one family member wrote in the late 19th century, "We go to Andalusia, more an old friend than a spot of earth."

HISTORY

Philadelphia merchant James Craig bought the property he eventually called Andalusia in 1795. The simple farmhouse was expanded several times, most notably by Benjamin Latrobe, first architect of the U.S. Capitol. After Craig died in 1807, his widow, Peggy, continued to live at Andalusia. In 1811 her oldest daughter, Jane, married Nicholas Biddle, who purchased the property after Peggy's death in 1814.

At the time of his marriage, the 25-year-old Biddle had yet to begin his long involvement with the Bank of the United States, but he had already traveled through Europe and fallen in love with Greek architecture, attended Napoleon's

150

coronation, served in London as secretary to James Monroe, edited the journals of Lewis and Clark, and been elected to the Pennsylvania legislature. Upon acquiring Andalusia, he threw himself into farming and for years served as president of the Philadelphia Society for the Promotion of Agriculture.

The Greek Revival "Big House" overlooks the Delaware River. Nicholas Biddle fell in love with Greek architecture during his travels in Europe in the early 19th century.

Beginning in 1834 Biddle worked with architect Thomas U. Walter to redesign and expand the main house in the style of a Greek Revival temple (it was named a National Historic Landmark in 1966). The Graperies were the main feature of the garden at this time. In the early 1830s Biddle tried several times to establish an outdoor vineyard before finally resorting to hothouse viticulture. In two huge south-facing greenhouses heated by coal furnaces, the grape vines thrived from 1836 until the 1870s. Later in the 19th century the struc-

One of many beautiful sculptures in the garden.

151

tures were damaged in a storm and had to be demolished. Only the two high walls remain today.

Biddle descendants lived at Andalusia until the 1970s, when they opened the property to public visitation. The late James Biddle, a great-great-grandson of Nicholas, wrote in 1976 that each generation made its own mark on the place without "irreparably altering a great nineteenth century landscape. . . . I hope you will find there, either in the house by the river, or in the garden, what we have cherished for so long in an ever-changing world."

The Gardens

The two Grapery walls are the most unusual landscape features at Andalusia. The long axis between the walls passes through a series of formal garden spaces, ending at the tower of the Reservoir House, once used to irrigate the gardens. Several gateways through the walls lead visitors from the formal space into the surrounding gardens, with a bed of peonies on the far side and shrub borders closer to the driveway.

The flower beds along the Green Walk, which begins at the main driveway and runs out past the Graperies, were first planted in the 1930s by Emma Meier, a nurse to James Biddle and then housekeeper and maid to his mother. This walk runs out to the edge of the woods, which are underplanted with thousands of daffodils. On the way

it passes a small cemetery with several permanent canine residents, including Schnapps,
Julep, and Brandy.

A pleasant walkway leads through a wide lawn
dotted with trees down to the Delaware River,
over three-fourths of a mile wide at this point.
The 19th-century riverside buildings include
the Grotto, Pump House (now used for storing
small boats), and classical Billiard Room (now
a private residence).

OFF THE BEATEN PATH

Andalusia's archives (open to researchers by
appointment) contain photographs, scrapbooks,
and other information relating to the history
of the property and the Biddle family.

Above: The yellow fall foliage of a Katsura tree (*Cerci-
diphyllum japonicum*).

Left: Large doorways in the
Grapery walls (the defining
features of this historic
landscape) lead visitors
from one garden area to
the next.

153

Bowman's Hill
Wildflower Preserve

www.bhwp.org

Surrounded by the residential development that has destroyed much of Bucks County's open space during the past 50 years, this 134-acre haven shelters nearly a thousand types of plants native to Pennsylvania and the Delaware Valley, including 80 rare and endangered species. Visitors who come to Bowman's Hill with open eyes will learn that the local woodlands are not an amorphous mass of "greenery" but a diverse habitat whose preservation is crucial to the ecological health of the region.

Native flora is the focus of the preserve; here, cinnamon ferns (Osmunda cinnamomea) uncurl in mid-April.

HISTORY

In 1934 the Washington Crossing Park Commission set aside 100 acres in the park near Bowman's Hill Tower as a sanctuary for native plants and as a living memorial to George Washington's army, which had camped nearby and made the famous crossing of the Delaware River just five miles to the south. Early on, Edgar T. Wherry, professor of botany at the University of Pennsylvania, began supervising the planting of as many Pennsylvania natives as could be successfully grown on the site. His planting records helped the preserve gain respect as a botanical institution. Bowman's Hill is the acknowledged wildflower preserve for Pennsylvania and offers a variety of nature-focused educational activities for adults and children. In 1997 it became a nonprofit institution, supported by almost two thousand members.

154

Map N2

1635 River Road (US 32),
P.O. Box 685

New Hope, PA 18938

215.862.2924

Hours: Daily, 8:30 a.m.–
sunset; visitor center open
9 a.m.–5 p.m.; guided tours
2 p.m. daily, April–November

Size: 134 acres

Visit time: 1–3 hours

The pond provides habitat
for turtles, frogs, fish,
and various aquatic and
moisture-loving wild-
flowers.

THE PRESERVE

Unlike other lushly planted wildflower gardens in the region, such as the Mt. Cuba Center, Bowman's Hill is not a planted garden. Visitors should not expect to find a profusion of blossoms tended by a staff of gardeners. This is a true preserve, a habitat set aside so that these plants, ranging from 100-foot trees to ground-hugging wildflowers, can grow and thrive in a natural woodland setting. Visitors are advised to ask the staff about the day's or the season's highlights and tailor their walk accordingly. A guided tour can help unveil some of the subtleties of this landscape, especially for those unfamiliar with the region's native flora.

One of the most striking displays at the preserve is the spring show of ephemeral wildflowers. These emerge and bloom early to take advantage of the light available before the trees above them leaf out, and then die back and disappear by late spring or early summer. The most spectacular are the sweeps of Vir-

155

NORTH

ginia bluebells (*Mertensia virginica*). Others are as fleeting as a passing thought, such as twinleaf (*Jeffersonia diphylla*), whose flowers last only a day or two. In other seasons, a group of native azaleas near the bridge across Pidcock Creek are beautiful in May and June. The Pond, reached from the Gentian Trail, and the Front Meadow, are colorful and lively in summer. The fall foliage is striking; and with two miles of trails, the preserve is popular for wintertime walks.

OFF THE BEATEN PATH

Bowman's Hill is a prime bird-watching spot, where about 150 species may be sighted over the course of a year. Bird walks are scheduled weekly from mid-April through mid-June. The visitor center features a window wall through which the preserve and its wildlife can be observed in comfort during inclement weather.

A bed of native plants located adjacent to the parking lot, the only cultivated garden space in the preserve, provides an example of how to use these plants in a home setting.

The Medicinal Trail and the Pocono Laurels Trail are among the most peaceful and beautiful on the property.

Mayapples (*Podophyllum peltatum*) are among the many native plants that carpet the preserve's woodlands in springtime.

157

Bryn Athyn Cathedral Gardens
www.brynathyncathedral.org

B*ryn Athyn Cathedral, built during the first half of the 20th century, is a landmark in the easternmost corner of Montgomery County, where its 151-foot tower stands guard on a prominent hilltop overlooking the Pennypack Creek valley. One of the most beautiful buildings in the Philadelphia region, this gem is finally getting the setting it has always deserved, with the ongoing creation of a series of gardens on the grounds.*

The design of both the building and the gardens reflects the doctrine of the Church of the New Jerusalem, an outgrowth of the teachings of Emmanuel Swedenborg, an 18th-century Swedish scientist and theologian. The cathedral and its adjacent academy and college serve as the worldwide center for the church. Although the grounds are open year-round, the gardens are at their best between April and October.

Opposite page: The Alpha-Omega Terrace—with Greek letters clipped out of boxwood—signifies God's presence from beginning to end, from first to last. Beyond is a view into the Pennypack Creek valley.

Below: This colorful container, with a tree fern (*Cyathea sp.*) in the center, is one of many horticultural adornments that surround this architectural landmark.

HISTORY

John Pitcairn, founder of the Pittsburgh Plate Glass Company, and his son Raymond supported, planned, and supervised much of the construction of the cathedral. Work began in 1913, carried out by groups of artisans similar to the guilds that constructed the cathedrals of the Middle Ages. Architects, stone and wood carvers, carpenters, metalworkers, and stained glass artisans worked in studios or shops near the construction site. The creativity of the individual craftsmen and their input into the design process generated a great variety of detail, reflecting, according to a church brochure, "the diversity of the Lord's creation." The main sanctuary was dedicated for use in 1919, while construction on other

sections continued until 1929. Some details of the building's ornamentation are still being worked on today. The transformation of the cathedral landscape began in 1991 when church member Danielle Odhner volunteered to work on the grounds. In 1997 she took over as head gardener. In addition to refining and expanding the beautiful gardens, Odhner is developing programs to teach people about the "botanical arts" through classes in gardening, beekeeping, and botanical illustration.

THE GARDENS

The architecture and ornamentation of the cathedral and the surrounding walls and paths, along with the dramatic hilltop setting, provide a backdrop that most garden designers can only dream of. Where there once were lawns, overgrown shrubs, and dying trees, Odhner and her talented staff and dedicated

Map N9

900 Cathedral Road (off Huntingdon Pike/US 232)

Bryn Athyn, PA 19009

215.947.0266

Hours: Daily, dawn–dusk; grounds closed occasionally for weddings and funerals. Cathedral open Monday 1–4 p.m., Tuesday–Sunday 9:30 a.m.–4 p.m.; guided tours daily

Size: About 6 acres

Visit time: 1–2 hours (gardens and cathedral)

159

volunteers have created lush beds with gorgeous color combinations using a variety of woody and herbaceous plants.

Five distinct garden areas ring the building, but they flow together so seamlessly that a casual visitor might not see exactly where one ends and the other begins. Many of the plants were chosen and combined to represent the teachings of the church. The East Border, planted in "fiery" red, yellow, and orange, represents a story from the Book of Revelation about a woman clothed with the sun. The Northern Shade Garden is the most extensive and beautiful, with large trees and shrubs shading a miniature woodland carpeted with perennials and bulbs. Here the predominant colors are shades of green, which represents "truth obscured" in the church's teachings.

A flowering dogwood (*Cornus florida*) sits on a terrace above a stone wall that is constructed as solidly as the cathedral itself.

160

The doorway to "truth revealed," the cathedral entrance, is located directly across the driveway from this garden. In front of the cathedral, overlooking the valley, several beds lie above and below a stone retaining wall. The south-facing Children's Garden, with pastel colors that are a testament to innocence and natural goodness, has become a popular site for baptisms. In the nearby Marriage Love Garden, purple-hued flowers predominate, representing the combination of red and blue in mutual love.

A long stone bench in front of the cathedral invites visitors to sit and reflect.

OFF THE BEATEN PATH

The inside of the cathedral is as beautiful as the gardens outside, and a tour of the building will help visitors better understand the symbolism of the landscape.

A long garden bed below the retaining wall, mostly invisible from the terrace above, is under development and worth exploring.

161

Meadowbrook Farm

www.gotomeadowbrook.com

Formality and whimsy cohabitate comfortably at Meadowbrook Farm. The rigid geometry of the garden rooms is a perfect foil for the eclectic garden ornaments, which range from a giant eagle with a six-foot wingspan to an array of lizards that lurk in the beds and climb the walls. Unusual pruned specimens—a specialty of Meadowbrook's creator, the late J. Liddon Pennock—are a highlight. The garden looks best in May and June, and again in the fall, when the warm-weather annuals are overflowing their beds.

Ferns fill every nook and cranny in this staircase, which provides a transition from one garden room to the next. The noble canines are among dozens of sculptures, large and small, placed inside and outside the house.

HISTORY

In 1936, when J. Liddon Pennock, Jr., married Alice Herkness, they received a generous gift from the bride's father: 150 acres in Abington Township and the money to build and furnish a house on the property. John Smylie Herkness could afford the gift, since he not only held the patent on carbon paper but also provided the ink used to print U.S. currency. The Pennock forebears, Quaker farmers from Ireland, emi-

One of several temple-like belvederes that serve as garden focal points.

Map N8

1633 Washington Lane
Meadowbrook, PA 19046

215.887.5900

Hours: May–November, house and garden open for group tours by appointment; several general open days each year. Display gardens (free) open during nursery hours, Monday–Saturday 10 a.m.–5 p.m.

Size: About 3 acres (includes house gardens and display beds)

Visit time: About 1 hour (guided tour of house and garden)

grated to Pennsylvania in 1685 and by 1714 had acquired 5,000 acres through a grant made by William Penn. One branch of the family eventually moved into the floral business, establishing Pennock Florist in Philadelphia in 1865. Three generations of the family ran the business until J. Liddon Pennock, Jr., sold it to its employees in 1966 in order to spend more time in his gardens at Meadowbrook Farm. In 1971, he opened a nursery there. After his death in 2003, he bequeathed the nursery, house, and garden to the Pennsylvania Horticultural Society.

The Gardens

Pennock designed the gardens at Meadowbrook Farm as the house was being constructed, and he worked on them throughout his life. Originally the house was to have been built right up to the edge of a steep slope, but Pennock insisted that the architect leave room for the two terraces that now provide much of the property's interest. The term

163

A small reflecting pool is surrounded by well-tended shrubs and small trees. Petunias garland the frog fountain; *Phormium* fills the urn.

The main fountain is the destination for several pathways. Topiary and other meticulously pruned plants are a special feature of this garden.

"garden rooms" tends to be overused, but it is especially appropriate here, as the hedges and walls that divide the outdoor spaces follow the same lines as the rooms inside the house. Touring the house thus provides an enlightening inside-out view of this delightful garden. Visitors will also see that the Pennocks brought the outside in, with flower arrangements, potted plants, and floral themes in the wallpaper, furnishings, and other decorations. Mr. Pennock's love of ornamental reptiles is also apparent, with scores of specimens inside and outside the house.

Staff recall that Pennock never ventured into the garden without his hand pruners, and pruned plants are a special feature here. Many beds are bordered with short hedges of closely clipped boxwood and barberry. In the courtyard in front of the house, a yew pruned into a cloud formation stands two stories tall. In the conservatory, seven old specimens of creeping

A lead eagle, weathered but fierce, stands guard over the upper terrace.

fig are trained up the wall and out over the space in a crisscross of living swags. Weeping hemlocks, kept small by regular pruning, flank the six-foot-wide eagle sculpture. Espaliered copper beeches, trained along a wall for 50 years, stand no more than three feet tall.

The gardens have several axes, with attractive features such as fountains, a belvedere with a wrought iron roof, the eagle, and several gazebos always in view, luring the curious from one outdoor room to the next. To some visitors it might seem too busy, too much, but this profusion is part of the garden's charm and, according to those who knew him, a perfect expression of J. Liddon Pennock's flamboyant taste and style.

OFF THE BEATEN PATH

Display gardens near the parking lot are less formal and more lushly planted than the gardens around the house, with a variety of unusual herbaceous plants, shrubs, and trees.

165

Delaware Valley College
Henry Schmieder Arboretum

www.devalcol.edu/Arboretum

Founded as the National Farm School in 1896 by Rabbi Joseph Krauskopf, Delaware Valley College still has strong course offerings in ornamental horticulture and landscape design. Besides beautifying the campus, the arboretum serves as an outdoor, hands-on classroom for horticulture and design students and provides the public with examples of good garden plants for the region.

In 1966 the arboretum was named in honor of faculty member Henry Schmieder. From 1921 to his death in 1964, he catalogued and expanded the college's plant collection, which now includes several gardens and a number of unusual specimen trees that are integrated into the campus fabric.

The Gazebo Annual Garden displays the latest annual bedding plants and vines. The Lois Burpee Herb Garden features more than a hundred herbs, and the Rose Garden includes both species and heirloom roses along with many of the finest modern varieties.

An iris collection contains many Dykes Medal winners among its 450 cultivars. Mature tree specimens can be found throughout the campus. The oldest, a sycamore estimated to be about 350 years old, stands guard over the president's house. Other old specimens can be seen on the Woodland Walk behind the Herb Garden.

166

GREAT GARDENS

Map N1

700 East Butler Avenue (PA 611 & US 202)

Doylestown, PA 18901

215.489.2283

Hours: Daily, dawn–dusk; visitors must register at the college's Information Center/Security Office, near the main parking lot

Size: 60 acres

Visit time: 1–2 hours

Top: Annual flowers grow in spoke-like beds around a central gazebo; diverse vines climb on the outer fence.

Bottom: The Lois Burpee Herb Garden features medicinal and culinary plants.

167

St. Mary Medical Center Healing Gardens

www.healinggardens-stmary.org

*I*n 2001 two longtime friends—Carter Van Dyke, a landscape architect, and Susan Wert, a businesswoman and philanthropist—imagined creating a small garden on the grounds of St. Mary Medical Center as a tribute to their mothers, both of whom had been treated there for cancer. This modest idea struck a chord with hospital administrators, who wanted to explore holistic approaches to healing, including the restorative power of nature. One garden mushroomed into a series of gardens, designed by Van Dyke, that have become well-used and well-loved respites from the human dramas inside the building.

Map N6

1201 Langhorne-Newtown Road (US 413)

Langhorne, PA 19047

215.710.2591

Hours: Daily, dawn–dusk

Size: About 1 acre

Visit time: 30 minutes–1 hour

The half-acre Cloister Garden is the largest of the gardens installed to date. It incorporates many Japanese elements, including a chapel-like seating area secluded by cedar fencing and bamboo and a small koi pond. Completed in 2003, the Cloister is always open and highly visible from the corridors and cafeteria that surround it and from the hospital rooms above.

The Emergency Room Garden, visible from the waiting room, incorporates outdoor tables and chairs for visitors who formerly had to use the concrete steps for seating. Other planned gardens include a planted courtyard opposite the Cancer Center and a rooftop garden that will brighten the view from the hospital's intensive care unit.

The Friends of the Healing Gardens hold regular fundraising events and recently purchased the nearby St. Mary Thrift Shop (140 N. Pine St., Langhorne, PA 19047, in the Pine Watson Shopping Center; 215.750.8400), using the proceeds to fund garden maintenance.

A traditional Japanese fountain calms this section of the hospital courtyard, providing a respite for patients, visitors, and staff.

NORTH

Tyler Gardens at Bucks County Community College

www.bucks.edu/tylergardens

*L*ocated on the edge of a modern community college campus, the Tyler Gardens are a surprising reminder of an opulent era now long gone and a tribute to the ability of a few dedicated individuals to rescue an abandoned, overgrown treasure.

Map N4

275 Swamp Road
Newtown, PA 18940

215.968.8286

Hours: Daily, dawn–dusk; house tours by appointment

Visit time: 30 minutes–1 hour (garden only)

Size: About 2 acres

The Tylers built an elaborate formal garden to ornament their estate, Indian Council Rock, which became the campus of Bucks County Community College. Here, an alabaster fountain sits among Siberian iris (*Iris sibirica*).

HISTORY

Over a number of years George and Stella Elkins Tyler bought up 2,000 acres along Neshaminy Creek in Bucks County. In 1930 they began building a 60-room French Norman Revival mansion on the property, which they called Indian Council Rock, a name associated with a nearby ledge overlooking the creek. Construction of the formal gardens behind the house began in 1931. George Tyler died in 1947; when Stella died in 1963, she left 200 acres of the property to Temple University, which sold it to the newly established Bucks County Community College. The mansion, renamed Tyler Hall, was renovated to accommodate administrative offices, and the barn and workers' cottages were adapted to college use. Unfortunately, the garden was neglected and went into a long, slow decline.

The Garden

Restoration of the garden began in 1999, spearheaded by college staff members Lyle Rosenberger, Barbara Long, and Russell Strover, who have been aided by a dedicated group of volunteers and the generosity of donors and area businesses. The garden encompasses four terraces that descend from the back of the mansion. The upper terrace

This grand staircase leads from the back of the house to the second terrace.

Above: A bronze figure by Stella Elkins Tyler is surrounded by a hedge of clipped boxwood.

Below: A wall fountain on the upper terrace.

features espaliered trees and an orangery now used as a classroom and meeting space. On the second walled terrace, boxwood hedges, gravel paths, and a fountain have been restored. On the third level, once the site of a swimming pool, the bath houses are now used to store garden equipment. On the lowest terrace a tennis court has yet to be renovated. Sculptures by Stella Elkins Tyler, whose Elkins Park house became the nucleus of Temple's Tyler School of Art, are placed around the garden.

OFF THE BEATEN PATH

Most of the Indian Council Rock estate was bought by the Commonwealth of Pennsylvania and became the 1,700-acre Tyler State Park, which adjoins the Bucks County Community College campus and offers many amenities (www.dcnr.state.pa.us/stateparks/parks/tyler.aspx).

172

Also of Interest

Pennsbury Manor, reconstructed on the site of William Penn's house on the Delaware River, has a small kitchen garden where heirloom crops are grown. House tours are

scheduled throughout the day, and various festivals are held at the 43-acre site during the year (400 Pennsbury Memorial Road, Morrisville, PA 19067, Map N11; 215.946.0400; www.pennsburymanor.org; open Tuesday–Saturday 9 a.m.–5 p.m.; Sunday noon–5 p.m.; admission fee charged).

The Lewis W. Barton Arboretum at Medford Leas encompasses the 168-acre campus of the Medford Leas retirement community. The grounds are open to the public free of charge daily from 8:30 a.m. to 8 p.m. Visitors are asked to check in at the Community Building (where maps and self-guided tour brochures are available) and to respect the privacy of residents. Guided tours are available by appointment (1 Medford Leas Way, Medford, NJ 08055, Map N12; 609.654.3000; www.mefordleas.org).

173

Community and Private Gardens

COMMUNITY GARDENS

Since the mid-1970s, the Philadelphia area has been home to one of the most active community gardening and urban greening programs in the country. Philadelphia Green, created in 1974 by the **Pennsylvania Horticultural Society** (see page 40), has nurtured hundreds of gardens around the city and provided a model for similar programs nationwide, including those in Wilmington and Camden. It also works with more than half of the city's 150 neighborhood parks, sponsoring, among other activities, "Spring Into Your Park" and "Fall For Your Park" seasonal clean-up days. The organization has helped "clean and green" hundreds of vacant lots in the city and has worked with the Philadelphia Water Department to develop innovative storm-water management projects on formerly

Above: Tomatoes and morning glories in The Spring Gardens, with a backdrop of Philadelphia skyscrapers. Since the 1970s, the city has been a pioneer in the community gardening movement.

Overleaf: Well-tended vegetables and flowers in The Spring Gardens.

176

vacant land. Its City Harvest project coordinates food distribution from the city's largest community gardens to needy families, with the vegetables grown from seedlings nurtured by inmates in the Philadelphia prison system.

Community greening conveys many benefits, one of which is an increase in the value of adjacent properties. Equally important are the spiritual benefits of these gardens and green spaces, which often provide the only touch of nature in otherwise harsh urban environments. In struggling neighborhoods these gardens can become a rallying point and a source of hope.

Besides the groups listed below, other organizations in Philadelphia, suburban municipalities, and several public arboreta have set aside space for community gardening plots. For gardening opportunities in your area, contact your municipal office or the county Cooperative Extension Service (see page 128).

PHILADELPHIA GREEN COMMUNITY GARDENS

These eight "keystone" gardens, among the oldest and largest in Philadelphia, are a sample of the many projects in neighborhoods throughout the city. Several of the following have been protected from development by the Neighborhood Gardens Association (www.ngalandtrust.org), which acts as a land trust, holding the titles to the properties in perpetuity. Unless otherwise noted, access to the gardens is by appointment only—though many can be viewed from the surrounding sidewalks.

Roots Garden at Fisher Park (Olney). This 5,100-square-foot garden within a park, built in 2002, contains herb and butterfly gardens and 26 plots used by 23 families and the science club and Boy Scout troop of a nearby

177

school. Their work has transformed a once-barren area of the park into a much-used and much-loved community asset (5th Stree at the corner of Fisher & Spencer Streets, 19120; park and garden open to the public; contact: Fisher Park Community Alliance, 215.685.2874–ask for community group).

Aspen Farms (West Philadelphia). Since 1975, Aspen Farms has been one of Philade phia's most successful and enduring community gardens, featured nationally on *Goo Morning America* and in *National Geographic*. The garden (28,400 square feet, 35 gardeners) serves as an outdoor classroom fc students from the Martha Washington Mid School. Solar panels supply electricity for th garden's three fish ponds, mural accent ligh and gazebo fan (4837–59 Aspen Street, 191? contact: Hayward Ford, 215.877.9354).

Summer/Winter Community Garden (Powelton Village/West Philadelphia). In 1976 the residents of Powelton Village crea this one-acre urban oasis in the middle of th Drexel University campus. Besides the regu garden plots, shared by Summer/Winter's 6 gardeners, student chefs at Drexel's Culinar Arts College use a 1,000-square-foot bed to grow and study heirloom vegetables (3233 Race Street, 19104; contact: Joe Revlock, 215.387.0341).

Liberty Lands (Northern Liberties). In 19! neighborhood volunteers transformed two acres of blighted industrial wasteland into a vibrant community park: Liberty Lands. Besides a vegetable garden and a mini-arboretum, the park contains two playgrour built by neighbors and a lawn area that hos neighborhood events, including outdoor mc

screenings. Liberty Lands is open to the public (913–61 North 3rd Street, 19123; contact: Janet Finegar, 215.627.6562).

Las Parcelas (North Philadelphia). The vibrant vegetable plots and flower beds, the outdoor kitchen, and the colorful murals and art objects of Las Parcelas reflect the Puerto Rican heritage of many of the neighborhood's residents. The 12,000-square-foot garden contains 16 plots. The Norris Square Neighborhood Project, a community development organization, uses the garden to teach children about their *raices*, or roots, and the importance of service to the community (2238 North Palethorpe Street, 19133; contact: Iris Brown, 215.634.2227; www.nsnp.com).

Hansberry Garden and Nature Center (Germantown). Created in 1985, this organic garden features more than 27 raised beds for vegetables and several ornamental beds, tended by 30 community gardeners. Covering about a third of an acre (13,970 square feet), it serves as an outdoor classroom for several nearby schools and involves other neighborhood children in activities including a 4-H program (5150 Wayne Avenue, 19144; contact: Vicki Mehl, 215.844.7344).

Recycled architectural features, including these two stone columns, give this section of the Summer/Winter Community Garden the ambience of a Greek ruin.

179

Like all community gardens and other urban greening projects, The Southwark/ Queen Village Garden offers neighbors a place to turn the soil and feed both body and soul.

Southwark/Queen Village Garden (South Philadelphia). Created in 1976, this 18,000-square-foot garden—the only large open space in the neighborhood—features flower beds, a varied collection of irises, an herb garden, a grape arbor, an orchard, beehives, and berry patches, in addition to the usual garden plots, worked by 74 gardeners. A mural commemorating the garden's 20th anniversary, created by mosaic artist Isaiah Zagar, covers a wall on one side of the garden (open on clean-up days, the second Saturday of every month; 311–13 Christian Street, 19147).

The Spring Gardens (Spring Garden). Besides providing 180 families with space to grow flowers and vegetables, this two-acre garden serves as a social center for the neighborhood. Children from several schools participate in garden activities. The original lot was once a neighborhood eyesore, site of drug dealing, trash dumping, and other destructive activities.

The Spring Gardens are now surrounded by a new sidewalk and a beautiful iron fence (1800 Wallace Street, 19130; contact: Stephen White, 215.236.2754).

COMMUNITY GARDENS IN WILMINGTON

Founded in 1977, the Delaware Center for Horticulture (see page 72) has sponsored a number of community gardens in Wilmington, including the following. To visit these gardens, contact the DCH Community Gardens Manager (302.658.6262).

Burton-Phelan Community Garden. This ornamental garden was created in 1994 on a vacant corner lot that had been the site of drug dealing and trash dumping. In 2002 Roldán West, a Wilmington resident, created a mural portrait of 26 neighborhood heroes. Among them are the garden's namesakes, community leaders Hattie Phelan and Dutch Burton (1001 North Pine Street, 19801).

Shearman Street Community Garden. Since the 1980s, neighborhood residents have grown vegetables and flowers in raised beds on this 2,700-square-foot lot. The site of educational workshops on many topics, it sits on land donated by the City of Wilmington to the Delaware Center for Horticulture for permanent use as a community garden (404 Shearman Street, 19801).

Valley Community Garden. This beautiful garden replaced three dilapidated rowhouses in 2001. Its 14 families grow a wide array of vegetables in 21 raised beds and donate excess produce to local restaurants. In 2003 artist Roldán West created a mural for the garden depicting the neighborhood's "Past, Present and Future" (600 West 8th Street, 19801).

Community Gardens in Camden

The Camden City Garden Club, founded in 1985, has created several community gardens in that city. It also reaches thousands of school-children through its Grow Lab program, runs job-training programs for young people, and provides jobs for youth at the Camden Children's Garden (see page 36), located on the city waterfront. To visit the community gardens or for more information, contact Mike Devlin at 856.365.8733.

Private Gardens

Gardeners are a curious and sometimes insatiable lot, always peering over and under things, trying to catch a glimpse of that hidden garden on the other side of the fence or wall or hedge. Besides the public gardens featured here, the region is home to countless private gardens, the best of which could fill a book bigger than this one. Here are some suggestions for locating and visiting exceptional private gardens in the region.

Founded in 1989, **The Garden Conservancy** (www.gardenconservancy.org; 888.842.2442) works to preserve outstanding private gardens throughout the United States. Its annual *Open Days Directory* includes several private gardens in this region.

The annual membership directory of the **Hardy Plant Society/Mid-Atlantic Group** (www.hardyplant.org) lists more than a hundred homeowners willing to share their gardens with other members. The organization also holds occasional tours of private gardens, in this region and elsewhere, as do the **Scott Arboretum** (see page 96), the **Pennsylvania Horticultural Society** (see page 40), and the **Morris Arboretum** (see page 18).

One of many outstanding perennial borders at Brandywine Cottage, the private garden of David Culp and Michael Alderfer (see description on next page).

Other private garden tours include **Bucks Beautiful Tour** (www.bucksbeautiful.com; 215.348.3913); **Philadelphia Open House Tours** (www.friendsofindependence.org; 215.861.4971); the **Shipley School** annual garden tour (www.shipleyschool.org; 610.525.4544); **A Day in Old New Castle** (www.dayinoldnewcastle.org; 877.496.9498); **Wilmington Garden Day** (www.gardenday.org); **St. Mary Medical Center Kitchen and Garden Tour** (www.healinggardens-stmary.org; 215.710.2591); and the **Gateway Gardens Annual Water Garden Tour** (www.gatewaygardens.com; 302.239.2727).

The owners of two outstanding private gardens have agreed to be included in this guidebook. These gardens are often featured on some of the tours mentioned above and are also open to group tours by appointment. They reflect the horticultural expertise, artistry, and irrepressible energy of their creators and,

while most floriferous in the warmer months, are worth visiting in any season of the year. Be aware that availability may be limited because of work, family, and other responsibilities. Please respect the privacy of these generous gardeners and visit only after making prior arrangements.

For more detailed information on these and other gardens in the region (including magazine articles and photographs), visit the website associated with this book, www.PhillyGardenGuide.com.

Opposite page: Horticulture is a family affair at Hedgleigh Spring, where three Cresson men have tended the garden for almost a hundred years.

Hedgleigh Spring

Charles O. Cresson
Delaware County, PA
610.543.6699

This beautiful two-acre garden, tended by three generations of the Cresson family since 1911, is full of rare and unusual plants collected mostly by the latest caretaker, horticulturist and author Charles O. Cresson. The garden has a historic feel, with an overall design influenced by the formal country estate gardens of the early 20th century, but on a more intimate scale.

Brandywine Cottage

www.davidlculp.com

David Culp and Michael Alderfer
Chester County, PA
610.873.1866

This two-acre garden surrounding a stone farmhouse built in 1790 features flowers in all four seasons, including hellebores that Culp both collects and breeds, an array of snowdrops, and daffodils that bloom around Christmastime. Other highlights include a four-square vegetable garden surrounded by overflowing flower beds, a walled "ruin" garden, and a richly planted hillside.

185

ACKNOWLEDGMENTS

We are most grateful for the generous support of the Chanticleer Foundation and the encouragement of its director, Bill Thomas, from the earliest stages of the project. The staff of Temple University Press, especially Janet Francendese, Charles Ault, Ann-Marie Anderson, and Gary Kramer, accommodated the unusual needs of this book with patience, humor, and professionalism. Thanks also to editor Jane Barry and designers Joel Katz, Mary Torrieri, and Kate Fabrizio of Joel Katz Design Associates.

Liz Ball and Rick Ray offered comments on the text and other encouragement. Theresa Trapp provided invaluable help in the arduous fact-checking process. Barbara Bricks, Phil and Jean Schumacher, Ilene Sternberg, Stephanie Cohen, Kim Brubaker, Denise Cowie, Eric Hsu, Barbara Klaszynska, Linda Mills, Kathy Mills, Pete Prown, Ellen Wilkinson, Frank Hayes, and Chuck Gale offered advice and support. Data on large and champion trees in Pennsylvania was gleaned from Scott Wade's website, www.pabigtrees.com.

Producing a guidebook of this scope and depth is a complex undertaking that has involved literally hundreds of people over the past two years. Perhaps most important are the many paid and volunteer gardeners whose accomplishments are depicted here. While it is impossible to thank everyone by name, we certainly appreciate the fruits (and flowers) of their efforts. The following people helped provide access to, information about, and tours of their various gardens: Michelle Anstine, David Atkinson, Brooke Barrie, Nancy Beaubaire, Margaret Bleecker Blades, Betsy Bowen, Mary Lou Carberry, Jenny Rose Carey, Deborah Cassidy, Rick Colbert, Mary Concklin, Dianne Cram, Colleen Curtin, Barry Cyphers, Betsey W. Davis, Lynn DeClemente, Mike Devlin, Elaine Early, Linda Eirhart, Hildy Ellis, Patricia Evans, Jeanne Frett, Eileen Gallagher, Grace Gary, Wendy Gentry, Rob Grassi, Todd Greenberg, Jeff Groff, Erin Harvey, Lori M. Hayes, Lori Hogan, Hillary Holland, Connie Houchins, Michael Johnson, Gerald Kaufman, Dena Kirk, Tom Kirk, Maggie Knapp, Tony Kravis, Margaret A. Krengel, Victoria Laubach, Bill LeFevre, Dick Levinson, Rick J. Lewandowski, Barbara Long, Anne Mattingly, Laurie McGrath, Steve Maurer, Ginette Meluso, Paul Meyer, Bonnie Murray, Danielle Odhner, Jane Pepper, Colvin Randall, Alice M. Randolph, Joan Reilly, Bill Rein, Suzy Rogers, Lyle Rosenberger, Claire Sawyers, Liz

Schmidt, Ian Simpkins, Kathleen Smith, Jack Staub, John Story, Patrice Sutton, Dr. Harold Sweetman, Jacob Thomas, Susan P. Treadway, Martha Van Artsdalen, Richard Vogel, Kirsten Werner, Susan Wert, Lenny Wilson, Jane Weston, Melinda Zoehrer, and Ted Zoltowski.

Special thanks go to David Culp and Michael Alderfer, and to Charles Cresson, who allowed us to include their private gardens.

Roy Goodman, Jane Alling, and Dr. Alfred E. Schuyler provided valuable historical leads and insights. Published works consulted include: John T. Faris, *Old Gardens in and about Philadelphia* (1932); Carl and Jessica Bridenbaugh, *Rebels and Gentlemen: Philadelphia in the Age of Franklin* (1942); Joseph Jackson, *Encyclopedia of Philadelphia*, vol. 1 (1931); James Boyd, *History of the Pennsylvania Horticultural Society, 1827–1927* (1929); John Francis Marion, *Bicentennial City: Walking Tours of Historic Philadelphia* (1974); Harold Bruce, *Winterthur in Bloom* (1968); Ben Yagoda, *The Scott Arboretum of Swarthmore College: The First 75 Years* (2003); Colvin Randall, *Longwood Gardens: 100 Years of Garden Splendor* (2005); Adam Levine and Ray Rogers, *The Philadelphia Flower Show: Celebrating 175 Years* (2004);

Firmly Planted: The Story of the Morris Arboretum (2001); Nicholas B. Wainwright, *Andalusia: Country Seat of the Craig Family and of Nicholas Biddle and His Descendants* (1976); Mac Griswold and Eleanor Weller, *The Golden Age of American Gardens* (1991); U. P. Hedrick, *The History of Horticulture in America to 1860* (1950); E. Bruce Glenn, *Bryn Athyn Cathedral: The Building of a New Church* (1971).

Unlike many illustrated books, where the writer and photographer may barely know each other, this project has been a collaboration from the start. Rob and Adam worked together to select the gardens, determine their placement in the book, and write the captions. Adam in particular is grateful for Rob's support through this long process, during which his role at various times resembled that of editorial consultant, cheerleader, and counselor.

Finally, Adam would like to thank Tom Borkowski, for his unending support and valuable feedback, for keeping food on the table and the home garden growing. Rob would like to thank Sue Leary for her insights, her laughter, and her love, which have sustained him through many long days. To these two we dedicate this book.

189

CENTER CITY PHILADELPHIA

FAIRMOUNT PARK

C16

C17

Philadelphia Museum of Art

EAKINS OVAL

Benjamin Franklin Pkwy

C18

Vine St

C19
LOGAN SQUARE

30th Street Station

SCHUYLKILL RIVER PARK

Schuylkill River

N

Race St

Cherry St

Arch St C20

JFK PLA.
LOVE PA

John F. Kennedy Blvd

Market St
C21

Chestnut St

Sansom St

C24

Walnut St

RITTENHOUSE SQUARE

Locust St

C22

C23

Spruce St

Pine St

Lombard St

South St

24th St
23rd St
22nd St
21st St
20th St
19th St
18th St
17th St
16th St
15th St
Broad St
Juniper St

Numbers in *italics* refer to pages.
Regional map inside front cover.